# Guided Reading & Literacy Centers

Stanley L. Swartz

Rebecca E. Shook

Adria F. Klein

Cinda Moon

Karen Bunnell

Marie Belt

Charlene Huntley

 **Dominie Press, Inc.**

## Acknowledgments

The authors would like to thank the many CELL, ExLL, and Second Chance Literacy Coordinators, demonstration teachers, and classroom teachers who assisted in the development of this book. As always, we are enriched by the opportunity to work with this dedicated group of professional teachers. In particular, the generous assistance of two of our California Demonstration Schools—Parkview, in El Monte, and Garfield, in Montebello—was appreciated. Foundation staff members Amie MacPherson, Cathleen Geraghty, Laurie Roach, and Nancy Rogers provided important support for this project. A special thanks goes to Janet Maule Swartz for her critical review and editorial suggestions.

Publisher: Raymond Yuen
Editor: Bob Rowland
Designer: Natalie Chupil
Photographers: Cathleen Geraghty & Cinda Moon

Published by:

**ℙ Dominie Press, Inc.**

1949 Kellogg Avenue
Carlsbad, California 92008 USA

www.dominie.com
1-800-232-4570

ISBN 0-7685-0196-2
Printed in Singapore by PH Productions Pte Ltd

2 3 4 5 6 PH 05 04 03

# Table of Contents

# About the Authors

**Dr. Stanley L. Swartz** is professor of education at California State University, San Bernardino, and Director of the Foundation for California Early Literacy Learning, which sponsors the CELL, ExLL, and Second Chance professional development programs. Dr. Swartz is the author of the Dominie *Marine Life* series, co-author of *Building Blocks of Beginning Literacy*, and the editor of the *Carousel Readers* and *Teacher's Choice* series, all published by Dominie Press.

**Rebecca E. Shook** is the Coordinator and CELL Trainer for the Foundation for California Early Literacy Learning and a Reading Recovery™ Teacher Leader. Shook is a co-author of *Building Blocks of Beginning Literacy* and a contributor to the *Carousel Readers*. She has been an elementary teacher and principal and a county office consultant. She now divides her time between training activities and coaching teachers in their literacy efforts.

**Dr. Adria F. Klein** is professor emeritus of reading education at California State University, San Bernardino and a Trainer and the Coordinator of ExLL and Second Chance for the Foundation for California Early Literacy Learning. She is published by Dominie Press and is the co-editor of the *Factivity* series, co-author of the *Building Blocks of Beginning Literacy*, and a contributor to the *Carousel Readers*.

**Cinda Moon** was a primary grades teacher for eighteen years. She has also been a Reading Recovery™ teacher and a CELL Literacy Coordinator. She is the coordinator of the West Coast Literacy Conference.

**Karen Bunnell** holds a master's degree in education and has more than sixteen years experience in elementary classrooms. She has also worked as a mathematics consultant, mentor teacher, and staff developer.

**Marie Belt** is a reading intervention specialist for the Fontana, California School District and holds a master's degree in education from California State University, San Bernardino. She has been a teacher in the primary grades for nineteen years and a CELL Literacy Coordinator.

**Charlene Huntley** has taught for over twenty years in special education and regular education, ranging from early primary to nontraditional adult classrooms. She has been a literacy coordinator for both CELL and ExLL.

All of the authors are Trainers for the Foundation for California Early Literacy Learning and contributors to the companion books, *Interactive Writing and Interactive Editing*, and *Shared Reading*, also available from Dominie Press.

## Note to Teachers

Guided oral reading is one of the most powerful teaching methods available. Good readers and struggling readers alike can be supported during a guided reading lesson. Teacher support can be adjusted to meet the specific needs of individual students.

Guided reading can be used in regular, remedial, and special education classrooms. Typically a small group teaching method, guided reading can also be used with an individual student in either a classroom or special setting. Guided reading is a classroom intervention that provides powerful instruction in the regular classroom. As an inclusion strategy, guided reading is an opportunity for regular and special teachers to support one another in a collaborative model. Guided Reading is also an effective teaching method for English language learners.

Step-by-step directions are given to begin using guided reading in your classroom. The theory that supports guided reading as an instructional strategy is also included in the procedures section of this book.

Teachers frequently ask, "What do I do with the rest of my class during guided reading?" The answer to this question is a carefully designed literacy center where students can work independently or in small groups. The section in this book on literacy centers provides many good examples developed and shared by classroom teachers.

Guided reading is direct instruction that helps students use phonics and comprehension to read and understand text. We hope that this book supports your work and helps you become a more strategic teacher.

**guid•ed read•ing**    \gīd•ed´ rēd´•dǐng\

1:  A teaching method in which students read orally and the teacher provides direct instruction in phonics and comprehension.

2:  A powerful way to support literacy learning.

# 1. About Guided Reading

Guided reading is an effective teaching method designed to help individual students develop reading behaviors and strategies that will support them in becoming proficient readers. The goal of guided reading is to assist students in becoming independent readers by supporting their use of sources of information to problem solve at both the word level and for comprehension of text. It is an effective way to specifically and directly support the literacy learning of both beginning readers and readers who are more advanced, and English language learners at all levels. Guided reading can be used by reading specialists, special education teachers, and as an in-class intervention by classroom teachers. It can also be used in an inclusion model. Special education teachers can have guided reading groups for struggling readers and students with disabilities in the classroom rather than pulling students out to separate rooms for assistance. The classroom organization, using small guided reading groups and students at literacy centers, lends itself to a collaborative model. Regardless of age, grade level, or reading level, guided reading can be used to increase reading achievement by providing teacher support to help students learn how to use their own knowledge and strategies to solve problems they are having with text.

**Guided Reading Is:**

*In general education, an in-class intervention for struggling readers and a method to accelerate advanced readers.*

*In English language development, special and remedial education, effective small group instruction and strategic one-to-one teaching.*

Guided reading **for beginning readers** supports the development of essential skills in phonics, fluency, and text comprehension.

Guided reading **for more proficient readers** emphasizes vocabulary development, advanced word analysis, and text comprehension.

An effective approach to reading and writing acquisition will include opportunities for students to be actively engaged in a literate environment, one in which reading and writing go on all day, every day, in and across all subject matter. This approach provides for the needs of all students, including

an intervention for those students who demonstrate a need for a more intensive instruction, including English language learning, designed especially for them. Guided reading serves as this intervention strategy. It is one of various teaching methods available to teachers to support students as they become independent readers. It is important to consider the reading process, the levels of teacher support, and where guided reading fits along this continuum.

# The Reading Process

Literacy acquisition is a complex task involving the development of oral language and the mastery of written language. As parents of more than one child can attest, children do not acquire oral language in the same way or at the same pace. Language acquisition is progressive, and it involves more than just modeling and copying. Students develop oral language by participating in increasingly complex conversations and extending their understanding of the language they hear and use. This is as appropriate for primary language learners as it is for English language learners.

The acquisition of written language, both reading and writing, is a similarly complex process. Students do not progress at the same pace or in the same way. Teachers have historically relied on various means to help students acquire an understanding of the English language system. Most students succeed in constructing their own understandings, based on the methodology used in their classrooms. Some students, however, need additional support in learning to read and write.

An approach to reading instruction that uses various teaching methods with different levels of teacher support, which is based on the student's own oral language and provides them with a means to develop their own reading behaviors to become proficient, is of greatest benefit to the largest number of

## Guided Reading for Beginning Readers

Students are learning to read and decode text.

Groupings of students are flexible, based on strategy use, text levels, or other criteria.

Groups are small, usually four to six students.

The teacher chooses a text based on student needs and reading level, and grade level standards.

The teacher introduces the text.

Students read the text orally during the guided reading session.

The teacher is present during all phases of the lesson.

Follow-up exercises may be assigned by the teacher.

## Guided Reading for More Advanced Readers

Students can decode accurately so that the focus is on vocabulary and comprehension.

Groupings of students are flexible, based on their needs and interests.

Groups are small, usually four to six students.

Students and teachers may collaborate on the selection of text.

The teacher introduces the text.

Students read a portion of the text orally during the guided reading sessions, and they read other portions independently.

The teacher might encourage student-led discussion of the text.

Follow-up projects might be jointly selected by the teacher and the students.

students. To provide this kind of reading instruction, teachers need to know what knowledge, skills, and strategies students already possess. Teachers also need a strong theoretical and practical understanding of the process of oral and written language acquisition. This understanding of theory and practice, together with ongoing and thorough observation of each student, is an effective approach to reading.

Reading is a cognitive process. Basic to the process is the understanding that what can be said can be written down and then read again by the writer or by someone else. Once the students grasp this basic concept, they must acquire an understanding of print—the code by which speech is represented as visual information—and the skills to decipher the code and turn it back into speech. In English, this visual information is composed of the letters of the alphabet, arranged in systematic patterns and clusters to spell words. Each letter has its own distinctive visual features, and each letter stands for one or more sounds by itself or in combination with other letters. Beginning readers need to learn to associate letters with sounds in order to access the information represented by print and comprehend the intended message. Comprehending the author's intended message is the goal of reading.

Readers at all levels bring their own knowledge and experience to the task of reading and comprehending what is read. Oral language and background knowledge are important resources that readers use to decode print and make sense of the message. As students progress through the grade levels to more challenging text, the language in books becomes increasingly complex; the language of books is academic language rather than basic oral or conversational language. This change must be part of their understanding as students become proficient readers and writers. Extra support is needed for students who are English language learners or who have low levels of their primary language.

## What Research Tells Us About Teaching Students

There is a considerable body of scientific research that identifies effective ways to teach students how to read (Report of the National Reading Panel, 2001). Five areas of instruction that are critical elements to success in teaching reading have been identified: phonemic awareness, phonics, fluency, vocabulary, and text comprehension.

### Phonemic Awareness

Phonemic awareness is the ability to notice, think about, and work with individual sounds in spoken words. Before you become a reader, you must be aware of the sounds that are in words. Readers understand that written words can be spoken and that they use phonemes or particular speech sounds when they read a word.

### Phonics

Phonics is the relationship between the sounds of the spoken language (phonemes) and the letters of the written language (graphemes). Phonics is a system for learning how to read words. The letters of the alphabet and their corresponding sounds, when placed in memory, are used to decode words.

### Fluency

Fluency is the ability to read a text accurately and quickly. Fluent readers decode automatically and therefore are able to concentrate their attention on the meaning of the text. Fluent readers recognize and comprehend words at the same time.

## Vocabulary

The words we know and use to communicate make up our vocabulary. The words we use when speaking are our oral vocabulary, and the words we can read in print constitute our reading vocabulary. Reading text with meaning relies on the words used being part of the vocabulary of the reader. A reader needs to know most of the words that are read to comprehend the text. Understanding phonics and using these skills to decode text is not helpful if the word decoded by students is not a word in their vocabulary, or if the meaning of the word can't be determined by the context of the text.

## Text Comprehension

The purpose of reading is to understand what is read. Comprehension is the ability to take meaning from text and remember and communicate the meaning from the text. Good readers are those who monitor their comprehension to make sure they understand the text.

# Reading in the Classroom

The development of literacy is progressive. The process of learning to read involves surrounding students with conversation and print, modeling how reading is done, providing direct instruction in specific areas of need, and encouraging them to engage in similar activities independently. Various teaching methods are available to provide this support throughout the reading process, including reading aloud, shared reading, guided reading, reciprocal teaching, book clubs, and independent reading.

## Reading Aloud

Reading aloud to students allows them to experience great examples of literature—works they would not be able to read on their own at this point in their learning—and to experience a variety of forms and styles of writing. It acquaints them with the language and form of books and allows them to appreciate the pleasure that comes from reading without having to concentrate on the mechanics of decoding the printed word. It provides access for all students and is particularly supportive of English language learners. Reading aloud encourages them to want to emulate the reader and to acquire the skills that will allow them to enjoy the pleasure and satisfaction of reading for themselves. The listening and thinking skills used during reading aloud help students with the development of comprehension skills that are used when they read.

## Shared Reading

In the classroom, the reading done with students is called shared reading. The technique of shared reading in the classroom was created to replicate the experience of storybook reading, where the student sits on an adult's lap and follows along as the adult reads aloud. Shared reading is commonly done with "big books" —books large enough to allow a group of students to see the print and follow along. Shared reading can also be done with poems and songs that are written on chart paper or used with the overhead projector and the products of interactive writing activities. The teacher's role in shared reading is to: 1) choose appropriate material, 2) point to the text while reading word-by-word for beginning readers and phrase-by-phrase or line-by-line for more advanced readers, 3) read along with the students, 4) read in a fluent and expressive manner, 5) select explicit skills for direct instruction, and 6) observe the students' responses and behaviors.

## Guided Reading

In guided oral reading, students assume more responsibility than in shared reading. The teacher and a group of students, or sometimes just one student, have their own copy of the book being read. The teacher provides an introduction to the story and then observes the students as they read orally, talk, think, and question their way through the story. The text chosen for guided reading should be within an instructional range and should permit some new learning and the opportunity for problem solving by the students. The teacher assists the students in the problem solving experiences in such a manner as to promote future use of the behaviors and strategies needed by students to become proficient readers.

### Independent Reading

In independent reading, the students assume responsibility for reading. Opportunities for independent reading should be part of each stage of students' literacy development. Materials for independent reading can be familiar stories that students know from reading aloud, shared reading, and guided reading experiences. New books appropriate to a student's independent level may also be used. The teacher takes this time to observe individual student reading behaviors and problem solving strategies and provides necessary support.

*Two other small group teaching methods are available for more advanced readers that use flexible grouping and where students apply reading and thinking strategies: reciprocal teaching, and book clubs.*

### Reciprocal Teaching

Reciprocal Teaching is an instructional approach that is used to help students read for meaning and monitor their comprehension. It is a small group activity that uses the major comprehension strategies of predicting, clarifying, questioning, and summarizing to encourage thinking during the reading process. This approach focuses more on reading in the content areas but is appropriate for literature as well.

### Book Clubs

Students who are proficient at using decoding systems can be organized into book clubs in which the books read are selected by topic and interest. Book clubs help develop comprehension strategies and overall enjoyment of reading. The teacher meets with the group regularly to discuss issues, clarify points, and extend student thinking while monitoring for progress.

## Levels of Teacher Support

These four types of reading instruction—reading aloud, shared reading, guided reading, and independent reading—can be thought of as plotted along a continuum. Reading aloud and shared reading provide high support from the teacher with low levels of student independence expected. Guided reading provides moderate support from the teacher with an increase in student work. Independent reading requires high levels of student independence, with students reading with understanding and problem solving using a variety of sources of information with low teacher support and guidance.

### Levels of Teacher Support and Student Independence

| Reading Aloud | Shared Reading | Guided Reading | Independent Reading |
|---|---|---|---|
| *Highest Support* | *High Support* | *Moderate Support* | *Low Support* |
| Teacher reads | Teacher models | Student reads | Student reads |
| Student listens | All read together | Teacher listens and prompts for strategies | Teacher observes and assesses |

The level of text difficulty is also a consideration in selecting a teaching methodology that matches the need for teacher support. These levels can be expressed as:

**Frustration** (or hard) reading level, where the student is able to read at 90 percent or less word-identification accuracy and less than 75 percent comprehension. Text at this level is appropriate for reading aloud and shared reading.

**Instructional** reading level, where the student is able to read with 90-95 percent word-identification accuracy and 75 percent comprehension. Text at this level is appropriate for guided reading.

> *The support level provided by the teacher decreases as the student's independence level increases.*
>
> *This independence develops through the skills taught in each of these teaching methods.*

**Independent** reading level, where the student is able to read at or above 95 percent word-identification and better than 90 percent comprehension. Students read text independently with minimal teacher support at this level.

The Record of Oral Reading is an instrument that can be used to establish the reading level for individual students (see Page 137).

## Guided Reading in Context

Guided reading is a direct instruction teaching method that provides specific support to students as they advance in their reading acquisition and develop into proficient readers. When students read out loud, it provides the teacher with a window on their reading behaviors. Understanding what students try to do to solve problems while reading text gives the teacher an opportunity to provide specific feedback through the use of strategic prompts. Students are prompted to use what they know or to use a specific behavior. **It is a frequent teacher error to provide too much help, or the wrong type of help, rather than too little.** Teachers should prompt students to use their own knowledge rather than rely on the teacher to provide the information they need. Telling a student the correct word at a point

of difficulty does not develop independent problem solving. Guiding a student to learn to problem solve through the use of appropriate prompts and with careful observation and follow-up is the most effective way of developing proficient, independent readers. Guided reading is most effective when the teacher uses data about students in the group to choose books and provide support that is consistent with the needs of the students. The informed teacher is an effective teacher.

## Benefits of Guided Reading

Provides an opportunity to problem solve while reading for meaning

Provides an opportunity for phonics instruction and word analysis

Provides an opportunity to learn language structure and grammar skills

Provides an opportunity to develop good reading behaviors

Supports the development of comprehension strategies

Provides an opportunity to improve fluent and expressive reading

Guides teacher diagnosis, instruction, and evaluation

Supports English language acquisition

*Guided reading* is a term reserved for the teaching method whereby a teacher works with an individual student or convenes small groups of students to listen to them read and provide specific support that helps them use strategies to decode and comprehend text. Students in these groups are similar in need and read text that is new to them. **Students read out loud, from the same text, at the same time, but at their own individual pace. They do not read chorally.** Teacher support should include an introduction to the text, prompts for problem solving during the reading, and the use of discussion and specific teaching points after the reading to enhance decoding skills and comprehension.

## Components of Guided Reading

The students are convened individually or in small homogeneous groups of two to six.

The students read out loud, from the same text, at the same time, but at their own individual pace.

Groupings are flexible by similar level and use of reading behaviors.

The students read a whole text or a unified part of a text out loud.

The texts are new and gradually become more challenging.

The teacher introduces the text.

The teacher supports the reading at points of need to assist with strategy development.

The teacher makes teaching points and encourages discussion of the text.

## 2. Getting Started

### Step 1

The students participate in various literacy centers developed by the teacher and designed for independent practice.

For example, some centers might focus on specific practice as reinforcement to a shared reading, interactive writing, or previous guided reading lesson. Other centers might have a content focus (math, science, or social studies) that requires the students to use literacy skills.

*Note: An effective guided reading lesson depends on the ability of the other students in the class to work in literacy centers independently so that the teacher can focus on the needs of the students in the guided reading group.*

If the teacher can sit in the middle of the classroom with all the students engaged in independent work at centers and not be interrupted by students with questions or problems, then guided reading can be initiated with success.

### Step 2

Students should be assessed to determine their individual strengths and needs.

*Note: Three resources are provided in this book.*

*First, a Literacy Skills Checklist (Page 132) is included in the Assessment section. The checklist can assist teachers in identifying and verifying specific skill acquisition for each student.*

*Second, a Record of Oral Reading (Page 137) is located in the same section. This provides the teacher with a method of observing and recording strategies that the students use in their reading.*

*Third, an Observation Guide (Page 139) is provided that can be used to record anecdotal information from various teaching methods. This information can also be helpful in determining student strengths and needs.*

### Step 3

The students are grouped for guided reading according to the results of the assessments. Guided reading is more effective when students are grouped according to similar needs.

Groups are formed based on various criteria, including reading level, interest, and specific needs. The frequency of guided reading will vary. Teachers might see their lowest students every day and their more advanced students only once or twice per week.

*Note: Guided reading can be effective one-to-one and with small groups. The number in the group can increase as the teacher becomes more proficient in guided reading.*

Groups of students should be located in a semicircle or in close proximity facing the teacher, with the teacher in a central location. This allows the teacher convenient access to all the students in order to support and prompt them during their reading. It also allows the teacher to visually monitor other students' participation in literacy centers.

## Step 4

Choose an appropriate text. The students in the group will read from their own copy of the same text and at their own individual pace.

*Note: Texts that are whole or a unified part of a text allow students to focus on comprehension. If the segments are too small, it is difficult for students to grasp the story concepts.*

## Step 5

Introduce the book. It is important for the teacher to read the book beforehand and think about those features of the text that might need discussion before planning instruction.

Preview the text with a focus on phonics and word analysis, unusual language structure, and unfamiliar vocabulary. It is important to help students think about comprehension strategies and how they can be used.

Help the students think about sources of information that can be used to problem solve. They should also be encouraged to monitor their comprehension of the text.

*Note: The purpose of the book introduction is to provide background information about the text. Focus on information specific to the book rather than general information. For example, if the book is about soccer, talk about soccer rather than sports in general.*

The teacher should use a conversational tone and encourage the students to share their ideas and experiences.

## Step 6

Ask the students to read the book. Instruct them to read out loud, at the same time, at their own individual pace, and in a soft voice. **Students do not read chorally.**

At first, listening to all of the students read at the same time can be difficult. Teachers will find that this problem decreases with experience.

If any of the students are reading too softly or too loudly, ask them to adjust their voices accordingly. If the students begin to read chorally, ask one of them to stop and reread a sentence or ask a question about their reading to break this pattern.

*Note: Listening to a student read out loud is the teacher's window into the student's reading behavior. Although teachers cannot attend to all students at the same time, they can alternate and tune in to different students, or listen for students who are having difficulty.*

## Step 7

Prompt the students to encourage their use of strategies. This prompting is a way to help them use what they already know to solve the problems they are having with the text.

Focus on an individual student when you hear an error, when the student hesitates, stops, repeats text, looks around for help, or when the student asks for help. Teachers with substantial knowledge about their students can anticipate problem areas for different students.

Provide an appropriate prompt based on the error or confusion that was heard. If the specific error is not picked up on, ask the student to try reading that part again, but do not make the student feel that rereading is required only because of an error.

Remember that the purpose of guided reading is to allow students to practice their reading behaviors with teacher support and prompting. A list of prompts that provide support at various levels is provided in the Procedures section of this book.

If some students finish reading the book before the rest of the group, tell them to reread the text.

*Note: It is typical for the teacher to try to provide a prompt or some specific attention to any student in the group who needs help. Sometimes the attention might involve praising students for successful problem solving or reading.*

## Step 8

Discuss the book and make appropriate teaching points. This discussion about the text should help the students think about what they have read and their comprehension of the story. A comprehension probe might be used to explore specific understanding of the text, or the students might be asked to retell the story.

You can make specific teaching points, based on observations of the reading. A teaching point might focus on a confusion exhibited during the reading that you feel might be useful to the whole group.

A general teaching point might be based on why the text was selected in the first place. For example, if the text uses a lot of dialogue, the teaching points might include the use of quotation marks, or how the language of the speakers is similar to or different from language usually used in a book.

## Step 9

Books used in guided reading are usually unfamiliar texts. After their use in guided reading, these books can be used in literacy centers or by individual students as independent reading.

*Note: The opportunity to observe students' reading behaviors and the strategies they use in trying solve their problems is best accomplished in text that is new and unknown.*

## Step 10

After the text is read, one or two students can be observed in rereading the text. This might occur on the same day as the first reading or on subsequent days. The teacher can use the Record of Oral Reading (see Page 137) to see which strategies the students are trying to use in their reading.

Independent rereading of the text for fluency practice and use of comprehension strategies should also be encouraged.

# 3. Guided Reading Procedures

## Before Guided Reading

Successful guided reading requires careful and specific preparation. Students are assessed to determine individual needs and to guide the establishment of reading groups. The room environment generally, and the operation of literacy centers specifically, ensure that the teacher will be able to focus on the students in the guided reading session. Books are selected to meet the needs of the students in the group, and the levels of the books are verified. Text features that might cause difficulty are identified, and the book introduction is planned and delivered.

## Literacy Centers

Literacy centers are developed to provide independent practice in reading, writing, listening, and speaking skills for students in the classroom when they are not part of the guided reading group. It is critical that the teacher spend time introducing each center and how it is to be used before putting it out for the students. Literacy centers are designed to be at the students' independent level so that the teacher is free to meet with guided reading groups uninterrupted. Literacy centers should be a reinforcement or practice of something that has already been taught to the whole group in shared reading, interactive writing, or other literacy instruction. Routines are very important in the setup of literacy centers so that the students know what is expected of them, how to perform the task, where to get the material, and how to access and put away the center. Accountability in the use of literacy centers is that the students know their job and perform it. The Literacy Centers section of this book provides numerous center ideas, along with procedures on how to develop and use those centers.

## Assessment of Students

The support that teachers provide during guided reading is meant to be strategic. Being strategic means to be informed about the strengths and needs of each student. What reading behaviors does each student have? What do they use when they encounter a problem with text? Do they have command of all of the basic skills of decoding and grammar? Do they understand specific text features such as a table of contents, or a caption under a photograph, especially when using nonfiction books? Do they use comprehension to understand the text? All of these questions are ones that the teacher needs to be able to answer for each student to ensure support that will help the students improve their reading performance.

### Purposes of Assessment

Determine individual student need

Form guided reading groups

Help determine book selection

Inform teaching decisions

Monitor individual achievement

Determine guided reading effectiveness

Teachers have various assessment instruments available for their use. Most schools have an annual standardized test of achievement in which reading scores are of great importance. The results of these tests are used primarily for the purposes of accountability. The data they yield are usually not specific enough to help teachers design individual instruction.

Information from classroom observation and assessment procedures is used both to place students in an appropriate guided reading group and to monitor individual student progress. For initial placement in a group, the teacher might have each student read from a list of high frequency words and then group them by their level of accurate response. A record of individual oral reading behaviors might also be used for placement in a group and then to track progress in reading achievement. These observations help the teacher determine strengths and weaknesses the students have at the current time and how instruction can be planned to increase their reading achievement.

## Establishing Guided Reading Groups

Guided reading groups should be homogeneous, focusing on students with similar needs for teacher support. Students in the guided reading group can then read from the same text, which helps the teacher to be more efficient in listening and prompting them. Guided reading groups should also be flexible and subject to frequent change, based on the teacher's observation of student performance during guided reading. Some students might be placed in more than one group for different purposes. In addition, do not assume that all English language learners should be placed in one group, as their needs will vary considerably.

Guided reading groups are efficient because the teacher can provide individual attention to students grouped for similar needs. The students all read the entire text and benefit from the opportunity to practice reading. The Assessment section of this book provides instruments that can be used to assist teachers form guided reading groups and plan their instruction. The Literacy Skills Checklist can be used to notate the specific skills, both basic and those used for comprehension, each student has mastered. It is a

### Before Guided Reading

Select an appropriate text at the instructional level of difficulty.

Prepare an introduction to the story, keeping in mind the knowledge and current skill level of each student.

Engage the students in a conversation about the story.

useful reminder of those skills necessary to be a proficient reader. A Record of Oral Reading with both procedures and a recording form is also provided. The Record of Oral Reading is used as a tool to observe and record reading behaviors during student reading. Information from the Record of Oral Reading helps guide individual instruction and can also be used as the basis for forming, adjusting, or changing guided reading groups. An Observation Form is provided for use in recording behaviors during reading and writing activities. This form serves as a reminder to record anecdotal information for future use.

A Guided Reading Procedures and Self-Assessment is provided to help teachers use the information they have about students in planning their guided reading lesson. Both procedures and focus on students' needs can be tracked and noted with this planning document. This self-assessment is a helpful way to determine effectiveness of guided reading decisions.

It is important to understand that good instruction is not simply providing students with the opportunity to learn, but that it also includes strategic support from the teacher at the student's point of difficulty. This kind of teaching is specific to what is known about each student, rather than general to what we think are the overall needs of a group or class of students. These assessment instruments can be used to learn more about the actual behaviors that students use in reading text and then in the design of lessons that will help the students become more proficient in reading increasingly complex texts.

## Book Selection and Text Leveling

There is a wide variety of sources of print that can be used during guided reading. The availability of multilevel reading material is necessary for use during guided reading. The so-called "little books" are a good source for this purpose. Basal reading selections, content area textbooks, children's literature (both fiction and nonfiction), and magazine and newspaper articles can be recommended as sources and used for different purposes in guided reading. Because it is expected that the students in one classroom will have various needs for a variety of reading material (level of difficulty and interest), any appropriate print should be considered a potential source for guided reading.

When selecting texts for guided reading, it is important to choose texts that will allow the students to read successfully, while also practicing and extending their skills and strategy use. Texts should be at an instructional level; that is, the students should be able to read the text with 90-95 percent accuracy rate. There are currently many types of texts available that have been given a reading level by a group of teachers or a publisher, based on specific characteristics of the materials. These leveled materials are very helpful and can assist teachers in choosing appropriate texts for their students.

There are many texts that have not been leveled, however, and it is helpful for teachers to understand the characteristics of texts that make them easy or difficult. This understanding will enable them to use texts that have not been leveled or validate a level made by someone else. When looking at materials to use with their students, teachers can use the following criteria to judge difficulty and appropriateness:

**Sentence/Book Length**
**Vocabulary and Language Structure**
**Text Layout and Picture Support**
**Text Type and Subject Matter**
**Word Analysis**

Students take on the reading process at different rates, based on a variety of factors. Guided reading provides time for small group instruction that can target individual student needs with direct instruction. This instruction can be very powerful if teachers group students who have similar needs. Because students progress at different rates, there are standards set for proficiency at different grade levels. Based on these proficiency levels, appropriate texts may exhibit certain characteristics by grade level.

# Examples of Appropriate Texts, K-3

## Beginning Kindergarten

**Sentence/Book Length:** Books for students at this level are short and usually range in length from five to 40 words. The students are learning the difference between the terms *picture*, *letter*, and *word*, and these texts may allow for discussion of these differences. Books that label pictures with basic words or phrases are common. Sentences are short and basic.

**Vocabulary and Language Structure:** Vocabulary in these texts is basic and denotes objects and actions that are familiar to most students. Sentence structures are basic and direct, and contain phrases that the students are likely to use in everyday speech. Words, phrases, and sentence stems are repeated.

**Text Layout and Picture Support:** Text and pictures are clearly separated. In many cases, the pictures are located on one side of the page, and the text is placed on the other side. Generally, there is one line of text per page. Type size is relatively large, so that letter differences can be more easily discriminated. Spaces between words are large and make it easy for the students to discriminate word boundaries. The font used resembles standard print in many cases. The illustrations clearly support the reading of the text. Photographs are often used.

**Text Type and Subject Matter:** Fiction and nonfiction texts are represented, but the subject matter involves topics with which students are very familiar. Possible topics include students' families, friends, toys, or school. Nonfiction selections include topics such as colors and shapes.

**Word Analysis:** Text is short and utilizes high frequency words that are repeated. The topic words that are unknown are ones that can be easily predicted, using the picture cues. Letter and sound knowledge, especially on first letters, may be used to predict unknown words.

## Text Examples

### Dominie Letter Book: Long a

This basic label book features a clear picture that directly matches the one word on the facing page.

### My House

The basic pattern, "I can see my _____." is repeated on every page. Students use this language pattern as part of their natural conversation.

I can see my window.

I can see my roof.

I can see my door.

My House

Jan Swartz and Adria F. Klein

### The Bouquet

In this text, the pattern changes on the last page, requiring the students to monitor sight words.

This is a red flower.

This is a white flower.

This is for you.

The Bouquet

Rebecca E. Shook and Jan Swartz

# Middle Kindergarten

**Sentence/Book Length:** Books for students at this level are short and usually range in length from 15 to 60 words. Sentences are still short and basic, but there may be more than one basic sentence on a page. Longer sentences may extend from one page to another.

**Vocabulary and Language Structure:** Vocabulary in these texts is basic and denotes objects and actions that are familiar to most students. Sentence structures are basic and direct, and contain phrases that the students are likely to use in everyday speech. Words, phrases, and sentence stems are repeated, but they are slightly more complicated and require the students to more carefully monitor one-to-one matching. More than one pattern may be evident per page of text.

**Text Layout and Picture Support:** Text and pictures are clearly separated, with more text being located on the same page with an illustration. Text placement remains consistent, so that the students can easily locate the next portion to be read. Type is relatively large, so that letter differences can be more easily discriminated, and the font often resembles standard print. Spaces between words are large and make it easy for the students to discriminate word boundaries. When more than one sentence occurs on a page, each line of text contains only one sentence. The illustrations clearly support the message of the text and can be used as a source of information when problem solving.

**Text Type and Subject Matter:** Fiction and nonfiction texts are represented, but the subject matter still involves topics with which students are very familiar. Topics still include the students' family, friends, toys, or school, with the characters in the texts often engaged in some activity with which most students would be familiar.

**Word Analysis:** Text is short and utilizes high frequency words that are repeated throughout. Though high frequency words are embedded in patterned text, the pattern shifts due to changes in the use of different high frequency words. Students have more opportunity to monitor their reading, using their known high frequency words to keep them on track. Unknown words can be figured out, using picture cues, language structure, and letter and sound knowledge.

# Text Examples

## Look at This

In this nonfiction text, the pattern consists of two sentences. Students must use return sweep when reading both lines of text.

Look at this.
It is an ant.

Look at this.
It is a feather.

## I Can Do Many Things

This patterned book features an example of a single sentence that stretches across two pages.

I can ride my bike        all day long.

## Water

Familiar water activities are depicted in this book. Though the text has a pattern, it is based on a repeated language structure rather than simply repeated words, and so it is more complex. Students must use one-to-one matching and monitor their sight words in order to read the text.

We take a bath in water.        We play in water.

# End Kindergarten

**Sentence/Book Length:** Books for students at this level remain relatively short (usually 30 to 60 words), but they vary in length, depending on the content and the amount of new learning that is required to understand the text. For example, nonfiction texts that allow discussion about features of nonfiction text may be shorter and use basic, patterned sentences so that the students can focus their attention on the unfamiliar features, such as a table of contents or glossary. Texts about familiar topics may have longer, more complex sentences.

**Vocabulary and Language Structure:** Vocabulary in these texts becomes more challenging and requires knowledge in specific content areas. This new vocabulary is supported by common language patterns. Patterns are still evident, but they can change up to three different times over the course of the text. Short, cumulative, patterned text appears, with support of high frequency words throughout. Words, phrases, and sentence stems are repeated, but they are more complicated, with some patterns extending across two or more pages of text.

**Text Layout and Picture Support:** Text and pictures are clearly separated, with most text located on the same page as an illustration. Text placement remains consistent. Type remains large, but spaces between words are less prominent. One sentence may extend over multiple lines of print on a page, requiring knowledge of return sweep. The illustrations support the message of the text but require the student to attend more fully to letters in new words, which are repeated in the text.

**Text Type and Subject Matter:** Fiction and nonfiction texts are represented. Topics for nonfiction texts still include students' family, friends, toys, or school. The content of the nonfiction materials is exciting or interesting to the students. This new content is embedded in natural language structures for support, and is tied to information the students already know.

**Word Analysis:** Text is short and utilizes high frequency words that are repeated throughout. Changes in patterns often relate to changes in the use of high frequency words. Words in the text provide opportunities for the students to visually analyze a word beyond the first letter, and to begin to use analogy with words within the same text and within close proximity to one another.

## Text Examples

*Tea Party*

There are repeated uses of phrases in this text, as well as a use of a variety of different types of punctuation.

Here is your tea, Teddy Bear.

Here is your donut.

I'll eat his, instead.

### I Love Music

This book is an example of a basic, cumulative text with a pattern that extends across two pages of text.

I like to sing.

I like to dance.

I like to sing and dance.

### Animals Have Homes

In this nonfiction text, the featured animals are outside a student's everyday experience. The sentences are short and use a natural language pattern to support the student's attempts to read the unfamiliar vocabulary.

Koalas live in trees.

Camels live in the desert.

### A Walk in the Park

Features of nonfiction text are introduced in this basic pattern book.

My dog likes the tables in the park.

Picture Glossary

ice cream:    tables:

pond:    trees:

Factivity Series    SOCIAL STUDIES

A Walk in the Park

Adria F. Klein

People, Places, and Environments

# Beginning First Grade

**Sentence/Book Length:** Books for students at this level are relatively short. They range in length, depending on the content and the amount of new learning that is required to understand the text. Text is continuous and may extend to the next page. Books at this level usually range in length from 30 to 75 words. Texts about familiar topics may have longer, complex sentences utilizing more prepositional phrases. Sentences no longer end at the end of the line every time, with some sentences beginning in the middle of a line, immediately following the end of the previous sentence.

**Vocabulary and Language Structure:** Vocabulary in these texts is more challenging and requires knowledge in specific content areas. This new vocabulary is supported by common language patterns. Use of proper names is more common. Repetition of words, phrases, or sentence structures is evident. If patterns are used, they are longer and extend over several pages of text. More extensive cumulative patterned text appears, with support of high frequency words throughout.

**Text Layout and Picture Support:** Text and pictures are clearly separated, with most text located on the same page as an illustration. Text placement remains consistent. Type remains large, but spaces between words are less prominent. One sentence may extend over multiple lines of print on a page. The illustrations match the message of the text but require the student to attend more fully to letters in new words, high frequency words, and sentence structures when problem solving unknown words.

**Text Type and Subject Matter:** Fiction and nonfiction texts are represented. The content of the nonfiction materials is exciting or interesting to the students. Much of the content relates to common social studies or science themes. Topics for nonfiction texts still include subjects about which most students are familiar. Narratives are carried both by the picture and the print, with stories having a beginning, a middle, and an end.

**Word Analysis:** Text is short and utilizes a variety of high frequency words that are repeated throughout. Changes in patterns often relate to changes in the use of high frequency words. Words in the text provide opportunities for the students to visually analyze a word beyond the first letter, and to begin to use analogy with words within the same text and within close proximity to one another. A variety of punctuation marks become more evident as dialogue appears. The students will need to determine the difference between the different punctuation marks and letters.

## Text Examples

### Lost and Found
Proper nouns, quotation marks, and commas are evident in this patterned text.

Daniel said, "I haven't seen your glasses."

Jason said, "I haven't seen your glasses."

Lost and Found

Philip Swartz

### My Best Friend

Figurative language is introduced to the students in this basic patterned text.

My best friend is as soft as a kitten.

My best friend is as fast as a horse.

My Best Friend

Stanley L. Swartz

### Smokie

The complex sentences in this text extend to a non-facing page.

then I wash her face.

I take her outside to play,

then I wipe the mud off her feet.

Smokie

Sue Van Heurck

### The Sandwich

This cumulative book extends over three lines of text and has repeated high frequency words and pictures to support the reader.

I like bread and cheese and ham and lettuce.

I like bread and cheese and ham and lettuce and tomatoes.

I like bread and cheese and ham and lettuce and tomatoes and pickles.

The Sandwich

Adria F. Klein

### Feeding Time

There are several changes of pattern in this text. The students need to use high frequency words to monitor their reading.

I feed a cow at my house.

Cows eat hay, too.

I feed a pig at my house.

Pigs eat corn.

Feeding Time

Rebecca E. Shook and Beverly Hoffman

# Middle First Grade

**Sentence/Book Length:** Books for students at this level usually range in length from 50 to 125 words. A variety of sentence structures and sentence types appear in the books, as sentences contain more descriptive information. There are varieties of both long and short sentences represented. Some sentences extend over several lines of print, and sometimes to the next page.

**Vocabulary and Language Structure:** Vocabulary in these texts continues to grow more challenging as it becomes more precise and descriptive. More adjectives, adverbs, and proper nouns are used, with punctuation that influences comprehension, fluency, and phrasing. There is less use of patterned structures, though these are still evident in some texts.

**Text Layout and Picture Support:** Text and pictures remain clearly separated, and text placement remains consistent. Type varies in size, with some remaining large and others becoming smaller. One sentence may extend over multiple lines of print on a page. The number of sentences per page varies, but ranges from one to five lines of text per page. The illustrations match the message of the text but are less helpful as illustrations become more complex and less direct in their relation to the text. The students need to attend fully to letters in new words, high frequency words, and sentence structures when problem solving unknown words.

**Text Type and Subject Matter:** Fiction and nonfiction texts are represented. Though much of the content of the books remains about topics or experiences familiar to the students, many books allow them to explore different times and places through their reading. Stories become more fanciful, and characters and settings become more developed and important. Different text structures, such as riddles, become more common.

**Word Analysis:** A large range of high frequency words are used in these texts. The students will need to use their language structure and understanding of the text to solve unknown words. Many of these unknown words contain a variety of common phonic patterns and onsets and rimes that the students will need to utilize as they problem solve. Common inflectional endings will be used more frequently, requiring the students to read to the ends of words and rely on their own proficiency with grammatical patterns. A variety of punctuation marks are used throughout. The students should be encouraged to track print with their eyes, and not their finger, in order to promote fluency.

## Text Examples

### Moving to America

In this book, students explore another time in history. The vocabulary is related to the historical context of the text, and sentences are longer and complex. The students can use their knowledge of common onsets and rimes to figure out unfamiliar words.

Moving to America

Jon Swartz

We pack our things
in large wooden boxes.

We get on a big ship
to sail across the ocean.

We are leaving our home
in Scotland. We are moving
to America.

## Bill's Trip

The students are able to use their letter knowledge as well as their knowledge of basic onsets and rimes to help them read this book. The illustrations support this effort.

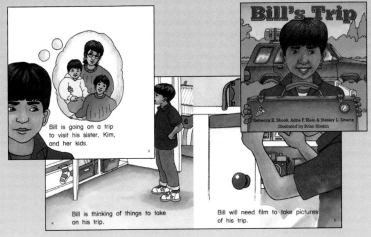

Bill is going on a trip to visit his sister, Kim, and her kids.

Bill is thinking of things to take on his trip.

Bill will need film to take pictures of his trip.

## Meet Mr. Cricket

Mr. Cricket is a fanciful character who is unlike any other cricket. The author describes him using descriptive vocabulary.

He wants to explore the world and become a great detective.

Mr. Cricket is not like other crickets. He is extraordinary.

**Meet Mr. Cricket**

Beverly Hoffman

## I Can Fly

In this basic riddle book, the students read five lines of text and need to use the clues in the text to find the answer to the riddle. They can still use pictures to help them read, but the illustrations are less supportive, as they contain more objects to consider.

I can fly.
I am striped, and I buzz.
I make honey,
and I can sting.
What am I?

I am a bee.

**I Can Fly**

Sarah Howard

## Mumps

A pattern is embedded in this basic narrative to support the students as they work with several lines of text, a variety of punctuation marks, and varying sentence structures. They also need to attend to inflectional endings as they read.

**Mumps**

Jan Swartz

It was morning.
"Time to wake up,"
said Mother.

"Oh no," said Mother.
Cathy had the mumps.

Her sister, Ann, was not happy.
"I hope I don't get
the mumps," she said.

Ann looked in the mirror.
"Do I have the mumps?"
she asked.

Mother looked at Ann.
"You don't have the mumps,"
said Mother.

# End First Grade

**Sentence/Book Length:** Books for students at this level are longer, usually ranging in length from 100 to 275 words. A variety of sentence structures and sentence types appear in the books, as sentences contain more descriptive information. There are varieties of both long and short sentences represented, and they are commonly arranged in paragraphs. In nonfiction texts, paragraphs about the same topic may go across several pages.

**Vocabulary and Language Structure:** Vocabulary in these texts continues to grow more challenging as it becomes more precise and content specific. Language structures that match the type of text used and go beyond a student's natural language pattern are evident. Vocabulary also matches the type of text; for example, "storybook language" versus content specific words. Because of these unfamiliar vocabulary or sentence structures, the teacher may want to address these issues during the book introduction.

**Text Layout and Picture Support:** Text placement may be inconsistent, with text located in different places on each page. A variety of sizes and fonts are used, with bold and italicized letters becoming more common. The number of sentences per page varies, but ranges from one to five lines of text per page. While illustrations match the message of the text, the text is too extensive for the picture to provide more than minimal support. The students rely more on their comprehension of the story to problem solve. In nonfiction texts, there is extended use of nonfiction text structures, such as a table of contents, headings, an index, a glossary, captions, and graphs. They will need to attend to these features in order to understand the meaning of the text and use nonfiction materials efficiently.

**Text Type and Subject Matter:** Fiction and nonfiction texts are represented, but with more text types included. The students explore fables, fairy tales, and journals, for example, and have the opportunity to discuss the characteristics of each. Stories become more elaborate, and there are more detailed descriptions of characters and settings. A wide variety of nonfiction topics are represented, relating to science, social studies, sports, or health. The students are able to learn new information from these texts as they decode print.

**Word Analysis:** A large number of high frequency words are used in these texts. Students will need to orchestrate the use of all their reading behaviors as they read the text. Unknown words can be figured out, using a variety of reading behaviors and sources of information. Instead of approaching unknown words letter by letter when visually analyzing words, the students should be looking for groups of letters that they recognize from other words they know in order to decode more efficiently. A variety of punctuation marks are used throughout.

# Text Examples

### The Three Little Pigs

In this traditional tale, sentences are longer and use the language structures common in literature. The text is arranged in paragraphs and may be located anywhere on the page.

### What Is Wind?

A science topic is explored in this basic text, which requires the students to interpret charts that support the information in the text. The illustrations in the chart help the students to understand the information presented. A picture glossary and an index are included at the back of the book.

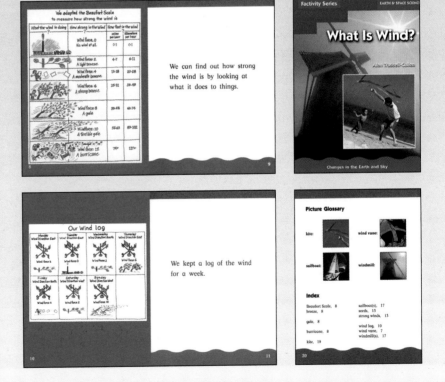

# Beginning Second Grade

**Sentence/Book Length:** Books for students at this level are long, usually ranging in length from 200 to 600 words. A variety of sentence structures and sentence types appear in the books, and the sentences contain more descriptive information. Longer sentences may extend over several lines of text, requiring appropriate phrasing. In nonfiction texts, paragraphs about a single topic may extend across several pages. As they read these longer texts, the students develop reading stamina.

**Vocabulary and Language Structure:** Vocabulary in these texts continues to grow more challenging as it becomes more precise and content specific. Phrasing of unfamiliar language patterns may need to be modeled to promote fluent, expressive reading. Language structures that match the type of text used are evident. The students will need to engage in discussions about how to use context cues in figuring out the meaning of unusual vocabulary. Vocabulary used also matches the types of text; for example, "storybook language" or content specific words. Because of these unfamiliar vocabulary or sentence structures, the teacher may want to address these issues during the book introduction.

**Text Layout and Picture Support:** Text placement may be inconsistent, and a variety of sizes and types of fonts are used. While there are still a variety of print sizes, as the size of the print decreases, the sentences extend farther across the page. The number of sentences per page varies, and there are one to eight lines of text per page. While illustrations match the text, they provide only minimal support. The students rely more on their comprehension of the story to use meaning as they problem solve. In nonfiction texts, there is extended use of nonfiction text structures, such as a table of contents, headings, an index, a glossary, captions, and graphs. Students will see several examples of these structures in individual texts.

**Text Type and Subject Matter:** Fiction and nonfiction texts are represented, but with more text types included. The students explore fables, fairy tales, and journals, for example, and have the opportunity to discuss the characteristics of each. Stories become more elaborate and feature more detailed descriptions of characters and settings. Students will have more opportunities to engage in discussions about character motivation and other literary elements as the stories become more complex. A wide variety of high-interest, nonfiction topics are represented.

**Word Analysis:** The students will need to orchestrate the use of all their reading behaviors as they read the text. Unknown words can be figured out with the use of a variety of behaviors, and they can discover which behaviors work best in various situations. Because the vocabulary is becoming more complex, discussions of efficient problem solving will be needed. The students will need to efficiently examine orthographic patterns in multi-syllabic words, being flexible in their use of these patterns and remembering to check their attempts against the language structure of the text and the meaning.

## Text Examples

### *2 of Everything*

This text has 217 words and requires the students to draw on background knowledge in order to understand the main character's feelings. Many words in the story are multi-syllabic and require them to use several strategies to problem solve.

### *The Farmer and His Two Lazy Sons*

The students need to use inference to predict the outcome of this basic fable, as well as to understand the significance of the climax.

### *The Grass Circles Mystery*

This basic mystery requires students to monitor their comprehension throughout the reading. The illustration on Page 13 can be confusing, so they need to pay attention to what is fact and what is conjecture in the text.

### *Cinderella*

The students' familiarity with this classic tale will help them as they problem solve longer sentences and complex language structures.

# Middle Second Grade

**Sentence/Book Length:** Books for students at this level are long, usually ranging in length from 200 to over 1,000 words. Most sentences are long and extend over several lines of text. Because of the increased length, most books at this level will not be completed in one guided reading lesson. The teacher will need to break the text into meaningful units. In nonfiction texts, topics are separated by specific chapter breaks or headings. As books increase in length, it is important to prompt the students to monitor their comprehension as they read, paying attention to key information and events.

**Vocabulary and Language Structure:** Vocabulary in these texts continues to grow more challenging. The students will need to engage in discussions about how to use context cues in figuring out the meaning of unusual vocabulary. As nonfiction texts contain features such as bolded type and glossaries to help them with unfamiliar vocabulary, the students will need to learn to use these adequately, with an emphasis on paraphrasing definitions, rather than simply reading the words in the definition.

**Text Layout and Picture Support:** Text placement may be inconsistent, and a variety of sizes and types of fonts are used. The number of sentences per page varies, and there are one to fifteen lines of text per page. While illustrations match the text, they provide only minimal support. The students will have to rely on their comprehension of the story to use meaning as they problem solve. In nonfiction texts, there is extended use of nonfiction text structures, such as a table of contents, headings, an index, a glossary, captions, and graphs. Though these text structures have been seen before, they are now more extended and contain more information. Students will see several examples of these structures in individual texts, often on the same page.

**Text Type and Subject Matter:** Fiction and nonfiction texts are represented, but with more text types included. Stories become more elaborate, with increased opportunity for prediction, inference, and higher order thinking skills based on the more detailed descriptions. A wide variety of high-interest, nonfiction topics are represented.

**Word Analysis:** The students should have a large sight vocabulary at this level that includes high frequency words as well as other words they have read often. They will need to orchestrate the use of all their reading behaviors as they read the text. Unknown words can be figured out with the use of a variety of behaviors, and the students can discover which behaviors work best in various situations. Because the vocabulary is becoming more complex, discussions of efficient problem solving will be needed. The students will need to efficiently examine orthographic patterns in multi-syllabic words, being flexible in their use of these patterns and remembering to check their attempts against the language structure of the text and the meaning.

# Text Examples

### Lucy, Plain and Ordinary

In this elaborated tale, the main character, Lucy the fly, goes through several misadventures before the tale is complete.

Lucy, Plain and Ordinary

Amber Johnson

Lucy envied the beautiful fireflies that flew and fluttered in the early evening sky. There was nothing plain and ordinary about them. Lucy wanted to be as pretty as a firefly.

The fireflies were very pretty, but they were also very mean and very vain. They teased Lucy and told her that she would never be as lovely as they were.

One day Lucy's good friend Rosey came to visit. Rosey was a ladybug who was always cheerful.
"You're looking especially sad today." Rosey said. "Is everything all right?"

Lucy explained why she was feeling so sad. Rosey thought she was silly for wanting to be like the fireflies.
"Lucy, you are always nice to everyone," Rosey said. "And you are the fastest flyer."

### Seals & Sea Lions

One topic extends over six pages of text in this nonfiction book that features bolded print, headings, a glossary, and an index. Because of the amount of new vocabulary, sentences are simplified.

Seals & Sea Lions

Text by Stanley L. Swartz    Photography by Robert Yin

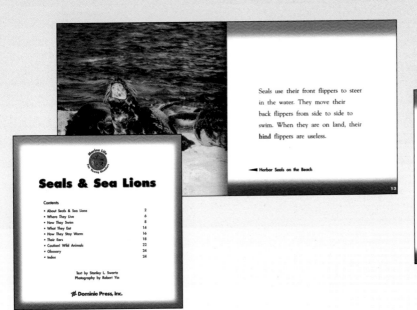

Seals use their front flippers to steer in the water. They move their back flippers from side to side to swim. When they are on land, their hind flippers are useless.

◄ Harbor Seals on the Beach

#### Seals & Sea Lions

Contents

Text by Stanley L. Swartz
Photography by Robert Yin

Dominie Press, Inc.

**Glossary**

beach:      The shore
blubber:    A thick layer of fat
external:   Outside
flippers:   Wide, flat body parts used for swimming
hind:       Back
mammals:    Warm-blooded animals
mane:       Long hair around an animal's neck
shallow:    Not deep
steer:      To guide
whiskers:   Long, stiff hairs
wild:       Animals that are not tame

**Index**

# End Second Grade

**Sentence/Book Length:** Books for students at this level are long, usually ranging in length from 350 to over 1,000 words. Both fiction and nonfiction books are commonly organized in chapters, though a chapter may be relatively short. As the students transition to these longer books with more extensive text, there may be a return to larger font and shorter sentences. Because of the increased length, most books at this level will not be completed in one guided reading lesson. As books increase in length, it is important to prompt the students to monitor their comprehension as they read, paying attention to key information and events.

**Vocabulary and Language Structure:** Vocabulary in these texts continues to grow more challenging. Dialogue becomes increasingly evident and uses colloquial expressions and language that mirrors ordinary conversation. Incomplete sentences and phrases appear in print as they do in natural conversation. As nonfiction texts contain features such as bolded type and glossaries to help the students with unfamiliar vocabulary, they will need to learn to use these.

**Text Layout and Picture Support:** Text placement may be inconsistent, and a variety of sizes and font types are used. The number of sentences per page varies, and there are from one to fifteen lines of text per page. Nonfiction chapter books will contain a table of contents as well as some pictures that are only minimally supportive. However, there are many examples of nonfiction picture books at this level that do feature elaborate illustrations. Even these illustrations, however, only minimally support the reading of the text. In nonfiction texts, there is extended use of nonfiction text structures, such as a table of contents, headings, an index, a glossary, captions, and graphs. The information contained in these resources becomes increasingly complex, and the students may be required to deal with several such features on any given page.

**Text Type and Subject Matter:** Fiction and nonfiction texts are represented, but with more text types included. Because texts are growing longer, the students need to develop ways to organize their thinking in order to remember important information. They will often need to use information from previous readings to support their understanding of new text. As stories continue to grow more elaborate, there is increased opportunity for the use of different comprehension strategies, based on the type of text being read. A wide variety of high-interest, nonfiction topics are represented.

**Word Analysis:** The students should have a large sight vocabulary at this level that includes high frequency words as well as other words they have read often. They will need to orchestrate the use of all their reading behaviors as they read the text. Because the vocabulary is becoming more complex, discussions of efficient problem solving are still needed. Students will need strategies to quickly use orthographic patterns while simultaneously checking their attempts against their comprehension of the text.

# Text Examples

## Baboons

The density of text on the page is increased, as is the density of the text in the glossary and index. The students will be unable to read this text in one guided reading lesson, and they will have to use information learned in previous readings to help them predict and understand new content.

### Their Young

Female baboons usually give birth at night. They normally have one baby at a time; twins are rare. A newborn baboon has a bright pink face, pink ears, and black hair. Its face and ears become darker when the baby reaches three to four months of age. By the time the baby is six months old, its face is the same color as an adult baboon's.

During the first month of the baby's life, the female uses one hand to hold the newborn next to her stomach while she is moving.

A baboon's eyes are open at birth.

## Story Cake

This narrative is arranged in chapters and contains the use of familiar ideas in unfamiliar contexts. The students need to monitor their understanding to ensure that they appreciate the nuances of the story. Picture support is minimal, but it adds to the understanding of unclear concepts.

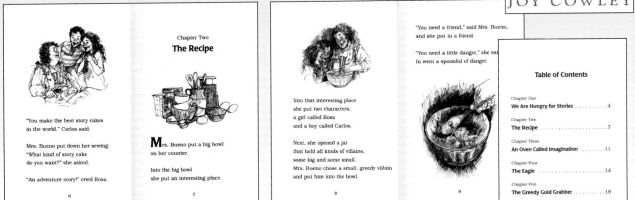

"You make the best story cakes in the world." Carlos said.

Mrs. Bueno put down her sewing. "What kind of story cake do you want?" she asked.

"An adventure story!" cried Rosa.

Chapter Two

**The Recipe**

**M**rs. Bueno put a big bowl on her counter.

Into the big bowl she put an interesting place.

Into that interesting place she put two characters. a girl called Rosa and a boy called Carlos.

Next, she opened a jar that held all kinds of villains. some big and some small. Mrs. Bueno chose a small, greedy villain and put him into the bowl.

"You need a friend," said Mrs. Bueno, and she put in a friend.

"You need a little danger," she sai[d]. In went a spoonful of danger.

### Table of Contents

# Third Grade

**Sentence/Book Length:** Books for students at this level are long, usually ranging in length from 350 to over 1,000 words. Both fiction and nonfiction books are commonly organized in chapters, with chapters that are increasing in length and complexity. Chapters in fiction books range in length from four to ten pages, based on the size of the print, the number of illustrations, and the complexity of the story. The chapters in nonfiction texts range in length from one to four pages, depending on the amount of new information and vocabulary contained in them.

**Vocabulary and Language Structure:** Vocabulary in these texts continues to grow more challenging, or may contain words used in different ways than expected. There is more use of extended dialogue, and the students will need to use punctuation to monitor who is speaking. Sophisticated language structures are used, in addition to language that is dialectical and adds authenticity to the piece. In nonfiction texts, quotes may be used to provide insight about the figures represented. The students will need to sort this information from the dialogue they are used to seeing represented with quotation marks. They will continue to explore features of text that can help them to understand unfamiliar vocabulary, such as parentheses, or definitions that are embedded in the text.

**Text Layout and Picture Support:** Text placement varies, and the students must decide which text to read and in which order. The size of the print is smaller, with more condensed text on each page. The number of sentences per page varies, and there are seven to twenty lines of text per page. Though full or partial pages may contain illustrations, the picture support is minimal, and many texts at this level contain few illustrations. Both nonfiction and fiction books may contain a table of contents. In nonfiction texts, there is extended use of other nonfiction text structures, such as headings, an index, a glossary, captions, and graphs. Photos with captions frequently add new information that supports the information contained in the main body of the text.

**Text Type and Subject Matter:** Fiction and nonfiction texts are represented, with a wide variety of biographies now available. Stories are more sophisticated, requiring increased background knowledge in order to fully comprehend the text. Higher level thinking skills are needed to appreciate the use of humor or suspense in a story. A wide variety of high-interest, nonfiction topics are represented.

**Word Analysis:** The students should have a large sight vocabulary at this level that includes high frequency words as well as other words they have read often. They will need to orchestrate the use of all their reading behaviors quickly and efficiently as they read the text. To aid in both pronouncing and understanding unknown words, discussions about root words, prefixes, and word derivatives would be helpful.

# Text Examples

### *Mailman Mario & His Boris-Busters*

The text in one of the chapters of this book extends over twelve pages. Longer sentences and a smaller font size make the text on each page denser. To support the reader, there are large illustrations on almost every page, which limits the amount of text on those pages.

### *Salmagundi*

Chapters in this book are shorter to help the students transition to reading text with few illustrations.

### *Thieves & Rascals*

This nonfiction book uses a variety of fonts on the same page, while some text is set aside in a text box. The meaning of the word *mimic* is embedded in the text.

### *Dr. Seuss*

This biography is arranged in short chapters. Photographs are incidental to the information on the page. Quotes are used to support information in the text.

# Choosing Texts for More Proficient Readers

As students become more proficient readers, and texts become increasingly difficult and complex, it is harder to provide characteristics that are all-inclusive. A readability formula is included in this book to provide a starting point for determining the difficulty of a piece of text (see Page 37), but teachers will need to use that information in association with the following criteria:

### Sentence/Book Length
- The length of text and its ability to sustain interest over time
- The number of unfamiliar words in each sentence or paragraph

### Vocabulary and Language Structure
- The number of unfamiliar words whose meaning cannot be easily determined from context clues
- An abundance of technical or content-specific language
- The sophistication of language used in the text
- The use of pronouns in the text that may make comprehension more difficult
- The use of language patterns that are unfamiliar (dialect, figurative speech, slang, etc.)

### Text Layout and Picture Support
- The use of columns
- The density of text on each page
- The amount and complexity of nonfiction text features (graphs, captions, maps, etc.)

### Text Type and Subject Matter
- Familiarity of students with the content
- Familiarity of students with the text type
- The complexity and sophistication of ideas presented in the text
- The need for interpretation versus straightforwardness of the text

### Word Analysis
- The ability of students to decode unfamiliar words in text

**Factors to Consider When Choosing Books for Proficient Readers**

Sophistication of the concepts presented
Student familiarity with content
Text layout and features
Vocabulary
Sentence length
Complexity of language structures
Text type
Length of the text
Probable student interest in the subject

When choosing texts for students at a more proficient level, a teacher must consider the general readability of a text, along with the factors outlined above. For example, if you are choosing a book that has a variety of nonfiction text features that are unfamiliar to the students, it is wise to choose a text that does not also have an overabundance of new vocabulary and complicated content. The students would be able to concentrate their efforts on understanding and using those new features of the text, as opposed to trying to attend to many new and difficult things at the same time. On the other hand, students who are familiar with such nonfiction text structures would be able to read a text containing more complex vocabulary and carrying more new information in varying page layouts.

## Readability

There are numerous formulas to determine the level of text reading difficulty. Some of these formulas are available on personal computers, while others rely on hand calculation. One of the most popular formulas is the one developed by Edward Fry (1977). Readability is established as a grade level, using sentence length and the average number of syllables of the words in the text. This formula assumes that the sentences in more difficult text are longer and that more difficult words have more syllables. In addition to these two factors, it is important to consider other variables that make a text more complex, such as language structure and vocabulary.

### Using the Fry Readability Formula

- Select a 100-word passage from the text. Count the proper nouns, numerals, and initializations as one word.

- Count the number of sentences in the 100-word passage. Estimate the length of the last sentence to one-tenth.

- Count the number of syllables in the 100-word passage. If you don't have a calculator, it is recommended that you make a syllable tally at the end of each line and then add the subtotals to reach the syllable count.

- Determine the grade level of this sample text by plotting the sentence length and the syllable count on the Fry Readability Graph (Page 38 and Appendix 11, Page 155).

- Repeat this procedure for two additional 100-word selections. Then average the three grade levels you obtained.

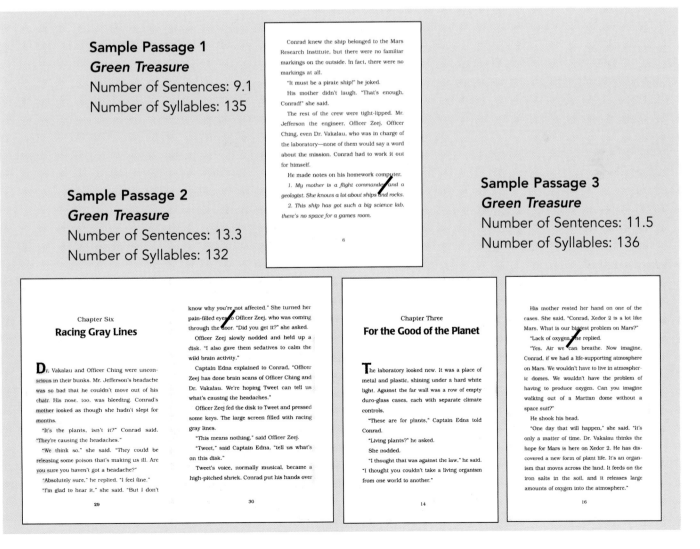

**Sample Passage 1**
*Green Treasure*
Number of Sentences: 9.1
Number of Syllables: 135

**Sample Passage 2**
*Green Treasure*
Number of Sentences: 13.3
Number of Syllables: 132

**Sample Passage 3**
*Green Treasure*
Number of Sentences: 11.5
Number of Syllables: 136

# Fry Readability Graph

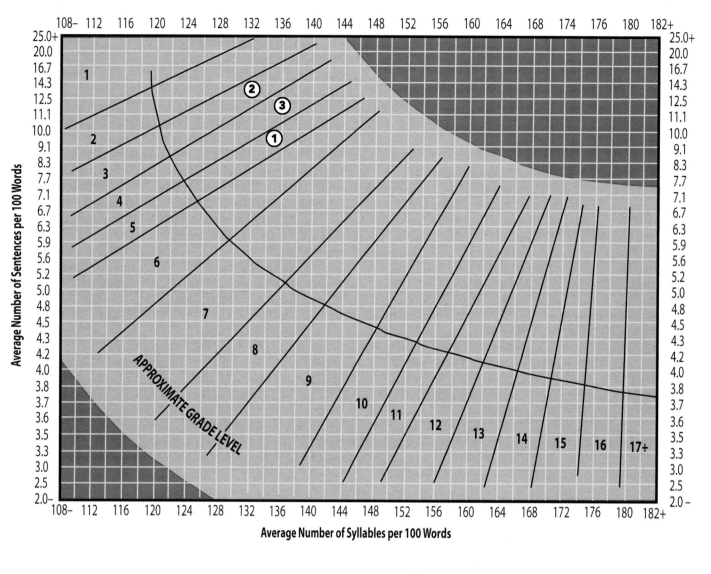

Sample 1 Grade Level: 5
Sample 2 Grade Level: 3

Sample 3 Grade Level: 4
Average Grade Level: 4

## Some Characteristics of More Challenging Text

- Stories are more complex.

- Settings, characters, problems, and resolutions are described in more detail.

- Sophisticated language structures are used.

- Vocabulary is challenging and may be related to content.

- Background knowledge and higher level thinking skills are needed to appreciate humor, problems, or suspense in a story.

- Picture support is minimal, though full or partial pages may be filled with illustrations.

- Print size is smaller.

- Some less familiar text types may be represented.

## Things to Remember When Leveling Texts

The criteria are general guidelines. Use these guidelines as you would a rubric. Texts should be judged based on where they fit best according to the criteria described.

Vocabulary is a key determiner of text difficulty. The more words in a text that are unfamiliar to the reader, the more challenging the text. Some texts are deceptively easy, unless you consider the complexity of the vocabulary. This factor is even more important for English language learners who have learned to decode but have limited vocabulary. Background knowledge, as well as interest level about a given topic, will influence a student's ability to comprehend text and is a factor that makes a text more difficult.

Generally, as the size of print decreases, and the density of text per page increases, the text becomes more difficult. The arrangement of text influences text difficulty. Adding features such as bolded print, columns, and captions makes a text more difficult. A greater number of such features in a text also makes it more difficult.

## Book Introductions

The book introduction is a focused conversation about the book. It is specific to the book that has been selected rather than a general introduction. The teacher talks about the language of the book, and the structure and vocabulary that are used in the book. The book introduction is also a conversation for enjoyment and sharing of common experiences that relate to the book.

The teacher prepares the book introduction in advance and thinks about the kinds of questions to ask and what difficulties the students might have in reading the text. These questions can be open-ended or closed-ended. Remember to keep the introduction conversational rather than a series of questions.

The book introduction for beginning or struggling readers might focus on hearing and using the language structure of the book and unknown vocabulary, in addition to the meaning of the book. More proficient readers might focus on strategies that will help them monitor their own reading and on comprehending the text to be read. English language learners might need to focus on vocabulary and concept development.

The book introduction is designed to help ensure that the students will be able to read with success and focus on their use of reading skills rather than struggle with unfamiliar vocabulary or content. What information is new to the students and what are they unlikely to be able to determine on their own? This task will be easiest if the teacher is well-informed about the sources of background information and reading skills of the students.

The most important consideration in the book introduction is that the meaning of the story be central so that the students can make connections to background knowledge. Remember that the purpose of guided reading is to assist the students in becoming more proficient readers. To do this, they need to

### Preparation for Guided Reading

Read the book.

Think about the needs of the students in the group.

Determine how the interaction will be conducted.

Consider the types of questions to be asked.

Plan and rehearse the introduction.

focus on the process of reading. The purpose is not to test the students, but to encourage their use of strategies and sources of information to problem solve and comprehend what they are reading. The book introduction helps provide background knowledge that the students might not have.

## Levels of Support

Introductions vary based on the amount of support needed by a group of students. Some groups may need high levels of support in which much conversation occurs before the reading of the book, whereas other groups may need less support to encourage thinking about the book. The purpose of any introduction is to give students opportunities to use their background knowledge in order to predict and discuss what may happen in the book. The teacher may use the exact language from the text as part of the conversation so that students have opportunities to hear, respond and use unfamiliar language structures and vocabulary orally before they read them in the text. This type of focused conversation before the reading of the text helps students when they begin to read on their own.

### High Support

Highly supportive introductions may be used for beginning readers or for students who need additional support with language, phonics, and comprehension. These students may just be beginning to use reading behaviors and sources of information in order to problem solve new text. Since their use of strategies is so new, the teacher supports their efforts by focusing the conversation on comprehension prior to the reading so that the students can devote their attention on decoding the text during the reading. Highly supportive introductions may also be used with more proficient readers when the text structure is new or there is a large number of unfamiliar vocabulary words or concepts.

### Average Support

An introduction for a group of more fluent readers who collectively have more reading behaviors and strategies in place would still provide the central idea of the story. The teacher would lead the students to parts of the book that may have unfamiliar vocabulary, language structures or concepts difficult to understand. The students may be encouraged to look through the book in order to develop an understanding of the story before reading it. Though the introduction would include less directed information, the teacher would ask key questions in order to help students predict and understand the text before reading.

### Book Introductions

Have a conversational tone—the teacher and the students talk together about the text

Allow the teacher to review unfamiliar vocabulary or language structures

Allow opportunities for the students to hear and use unfamiliar language structures

Provide an opportunity to support comprehension

### Low Support

An introduction that provides a low amount of support may include the teacher reading the title of the book and giving a brief summary of the text. The teacher asks the students to look through the book independently and uses students' comments to structure a conversation about the book.

The students may be asked to make predictions and to read for a specific purpose based on a small amount of information.

Examples of book introductions with varying levels of teacher support for the same text are provided.

# Sample Introductions

### Example 1 *This Game*

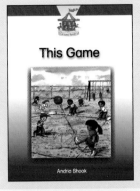

#### High Support

The teacher shows the cover to the group of students.

"This book is about all the different games that are played with balls of different colors. The title of this book is *This Game*, and each page of the story begins with those words: 'This game…'"

"Let's look at the pages in this book and see the different colors of balls that are used in each game."

This game is played with a red ball. 3

This game is played with a white ball. 4

This game is played with a brown ball. 5

This game is played with a yellow ball. 6

This game is played with a black ball. 7

This game is played with a blue ball. 8

This game is played with an orange ball. 9

This game is played with many balls. 10

## Average Support

"The book, *This Game*, is about games that are played with many colors of balls. Let's look at the pictures to see the colors of the balls."

As students share what they see in the pictures, draw their attention to the colors of the different balls throughout the book.

**Page 10**
"Oh look! This game is played with many colors of balls."

## Low Support

The book, *This Game*, is about games that are played with different balls. Look at the pictures to see the colors of the different balls."

As students look through the pictures on their own, encourage conversation about what they see.

## Example 2  *Ted's Letter*

## High Support

**Cover**

"The name of this book is *Ted's Letter*. Why do people write letters?"

**Page 3**

Ted wanted to write a letter to Jennifer.

"In this book, Ted wants to write a letter to his friend Jennifer. He is thinking about writing to her. How can you tell?"

**Pages 4-5**

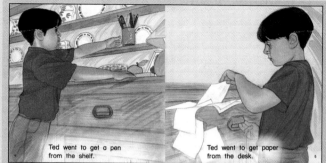

Ted went to get a pen from the shelf.

Ted went to get paper from the desk.

"Ted needs some things in order to write his letter, so he goes to get them. What does he get from the shelf? What does he get from the desk?"

**Pages 6-7**

Ted used the pen to write a letter to Jennifer.

Ted wanted to tell Jennifer about his new pet.

"What does Ted use to write a letter to Jennifer?"

"He is writing to Jennifer to tell her about his new pet. What is he thinking about? I wonder what that has to do with his new pet. I wonder what kind of pet he has. What do you think?"

**Pages 8-9**

Ted put a red stamp on the envelope.

Ted left the house and went down the street to send the letter to Jennifer.

"Ted finished his letter, and he needs to get it ready to mail to Jennifer. What does he need to put on the envelope?"

"Once Ted was finished, he left his house and went down the street to send his letter."

**Page 10**

Then Ted went home and fed his new pet, the red hen.

"When he went home, he fed his new pet. What is it? Is that what you thought it would be?"

## Average Support

"In this book, *Ted's Letter*, Ted wants to write to his friend Jennifer to tell her about his new pet. What might he need to use to write his letter?"

**Pages 4-5**
"Ted goes to get the things he needs. He goes to the desk and the shelf."

**Page 7**
"Ted is thinking about his new pet as he writes to Jennifer. What is he thinking about? I wonder what that has to do with his new pet. What could his new pet be?"

**Pages 8-9**
"When Ted was finished with his letter, what did he have to do before he left the house to mail the letter? After he sent his letter, he came back home to feed his pet. Let's read to see what kind of pet Ted has."

## Low Support

"In this story, *Ted's Letter*, Ted wants to write a letter to his friend Jennifer to tell her all about his new pet. When he writes his letter, what kinds of things does he need to do? What kind of pet do you think he might have? Let's look at the clues that the author and the illustrator give us about Ted's pet."

**Page 7**
"What is Ted thinking about? Based on this, I wonder what kind of pet Ted has. What makes you think so? Let's read the book to find out if our predictions about Ted's pet are correct."

## Example 3 *Sunshine, The Black Cat*

### High Support

**Cover**

"Today we are going to read a story about two older people who have a pet that they love very much. His name is Sunshine, and he is a black cat. Look at the cover of the book. The title of this book is *Sunshine, the Black Cat*. This is Grandma and Grandpa. Do your grandparents live near you? Do they have any pets?"

Encourage conversation about how playful pets can be and the kinds of trouble they can get into.

"In this story, we are going to see how Sunshine is a playful cat that sometimes gets into trouble."

**Page 3**

Grandma had a new cat. "We will name him Sunshine because he makes grandma feel good," said grandpa.

"Grandma and Grandpa have a new cat. They name him Sunshine because he makes Grandma feel good."

**Pages 4-5**

Sunshine was a playful cat. Sometimes he got into trouble.

He played with the paper. "Sunshine, stay out of the wastepaper basket!" said grandma.

"Sunshine is very playful. He plays with things that sometimes get him into trouble. Look at the pictures. What do you think Grandma is saying to Sunshine?"

**Pages 6-7**

Sunshine climbed on the screens. "Get down, Sunshine!" said grandpa.

Sunshine tried to help rake the lawn. He liked to jump in the leaves.

"Look at Sunshine. He should not climb on the screen. What do you think Grandpa said to Sunshine?"

"Sometimes Sunshine tried to help Grandma. How did Sunshine try to help with the lawn?"

**Pages 8-9**

Sunshine tried to help with the laundry. He liked to hide in the basket.

One day, Sunshine was lost. "Where is Sunshine?" asked grandma. They looked under the table and in the basket.

"Sunshine even tried to help with the laundry."

"What are Grandma and Grandpa doing in this picture? How does the thinking bubble help you know what they are doing?"

**Pages 10-11**

They looked in the kitchen and in the closet. "Here, Sunshine," called grandpa.

"Do you hear that meow?" asked grandma. "It is coming from the laundry room."

"Grandma and Grandpa looked everywhere for Sunshine. They called for him as they looked in many places. The picture shows you where they looked. Where did they look?"

"Grandma and Grandpa finally heard a meow in the laundry room. What do you think they will find when they look in the laundry room?"

**Page 12**

Grandma opened the dryer, and out jumped Sunshine. He was so glad to see grandma and grandpa.

"Where was Sunshine hiding? I am sure that Sunshine is glad to be out of the dryer.

Now you read the story, *Sunshine, the Black Cat*, and think about what happens to him."

## Average Support

**Book cover**

"In this story, *Sunshine, the Black Cat,* Sunshine is a playful cat. Sunshine likes to try to help Grandma and Grandpa, but sometimes he gets into trouble. What are some things that you know cats like to do that may get them into trouble?"

Encourage conversation from the students.

"Let's look at some of the pages in this book and see what Sunshine tried to do."

The teacher may choose specific pages for the students to preview and discuss before the reading.

**Page 6**

"Has your cat ever climbed a screen? What would you say to him if he did?"

**Page 8**

"Is Sunshine being helpful here? Where does he like to hide?"

**Page 9**

"Look at the picture on this page. What does the thinking bubble tell you about what is happening?"

Discuss this feature and take predictions from the students about what has happened to Sunshine.

"Now read the story, *Sunshine, the Black Cat,* and think about how Sunshine got into trouble."

## Low Support

**Book cover**

"Grandma and Grandpa have a new cat, and his name is Sunshine. Sunshine is a playful cat that sometimes gets into trouble. Read to see what kinds of things Sunshine does to get into trouble."

The teacher may ask the students to look through the book prior to the reading and respond to their ideas about how Sunshine gets into trouble.

## Example 4  *Lady with the Lamp: The Florence Nightingale Story*
### High Support

**Cover**

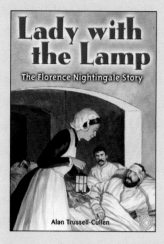

The teacher begins by reading the title of the book and displaying the cover, which shows a woman dressed in old-fashioned clothing and holding a lamp over some men who are bandaged and in bed.

The teacher tells the students that the book is a biography, which is a story about a person's life. The teacher directs the students to look at the back of the book, which contains a summary of the story. The teacher explains that this is a synopsis of the book and that reading it will help the students make predictions about the contents of the book while enabling them to determine if they would be interested in reading the book as an independent selection.

The teacher directs the students to follow along as the teacher reads the summary aloud, clarifying any unfamiliar terms or ideas. The teacher then directs the students to talk about what they already know about the contents of the book, based on their review of the front and back covers and the knowledge that it is a biography.

**Table of Contents**

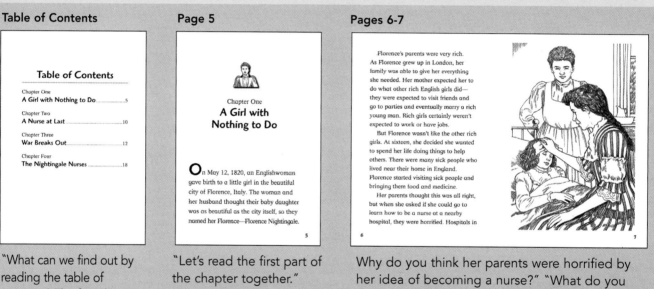

"What can we find out by reading the table of contents? The first chapter is entitled "A Girl with Nothing to Do." Based on what we already know, what do you think the author will tell us in this chapter?"

**Page 5**

"Let's read the first part of the chapter together."

"What do we know so far about the subject of this biography of Florence Nightingale?"

**Pages 6-7**

Why do you think her parents were horrified by her idea of becoming a nurse?" "What do you think *horrified* means in this story?"

**Pages 8-9**

"If your parents did not want you to do something, what might they do to discourage you?"

Write *Kaiserwerth Institute* on a white board or large sheet of paper. "Florence visited this school for nurses."

"Let's read the text and think about Florence Nightingale and what we can learn about her as we read this chapter entitled 'The Girl with Nothing to Do.'"

## Average Support

### Cover

"We are going to be reading this biography about Florence Nightingale over the next few days. What is a biography, and what would you expect to find out as you read one?"

"How can we find out more about the contents of this book?"

"Let's talk about what we already know. Does anyone know anything about Florence Nightingale? What can we tell by looking at the cover?"

"Let's read the summary on the back together and see what other information we can discover."

### Table of Contents

"What can we find out by reading the table of contents? What is the title of the first chapter? Based on what we already know, what can we predict about what the author will tell us in the first chapter?"

### Pages 6-7

"How do you think Florence's life may have been different from our lives?"

"Let's read to find out more about Florence Nightingale and how her parents reacted to her determination to become a nurse."

At the end of each chapter, the students and the teacher may discuss what they have read so far, clarifying their understanding and making new predictions.

## Low Support

### Book cover

As the students look at the cover of the book, the teacher asks them to read the title and make a prediction as to the text type and contents.

The students are encouraged to share any background knowledge they have about either the contents or the text type. After this, the teacher encourages the students to share other ways to gather information about the book's contents. As the students share various ways of gathering information, the group will look at the table of contents and make predictions about the contents of the text.

"In this biography, *Lady with the Lamp: The Florence Nightingale Story*, the author tells about the life of a famous person, Florence Nightingale. What is the title of the first chapter? What do you think the author will tell us in this chapter?"

"How do you think things may have been different in those days? What kinds of things do you think rich girls did?"

"As you read the first chapter, think about how Florence Nightingale was different from other rich girls of her time, and how her parents felt about her different ideas."

## During Guided Reading

The guided reading group, which is comprised of students with similar needs, is convened in a classroom setting. The rest of the students are working in literacy centers. In a special education or remedial reading room, other students might work independently or with an aide. The students are seated in close proximity to the teacher to ensure his or her ability to listen to the students read and monitor their reading behaviors. This might be at a table or in individual desks pulled together. Some teachers of smaller students might prefer to convene the group on the floor. The teacher should face the students and be able to see the activity in the literacy centers and the rest of the classroom.

Guided reading has various functions in the typical classroom. It is an effective method to provide direct instruction to students at all achievement levels. It is used as an in-class intervention for students who are having difficulty. And it is effective with the most advanced students. Grouping by similar need makes these multiple functions possible.

### During Guided Reading

Listen in and observe the readers' problem solving behaviors.

Prompt the students to use various problem solving behaviors.

Confirm successes and assist with difficulties.

Keep notes and records about the students' attempts and progress.

### Special Services and Classroom Collaboration

Supports collaborative planning and teaching

Uses an in-class rather than a pull-out model

Aligns teaching methods

Is an effective inclusion model

### The Collaborative Model

Classroom organization using guided reading and literacy centers is an effective way to use a collaborative model of service delivery for special education and remedial reading. This model provides an opportunity for two teachers to work in the same classroom with supportive but distinct roles. It gives students with greater needs more support and practice opportunity under a teacher's guidance.

The classroom teacher convenes a guided reading group and sends the rest of the students to literacy centers. During this time period, the special education or remedial reading teacher can work in the classroom and convene an additional group for guided reading or work in existing literacy centers with groups selected by need and/or disability. The special teacher might also choose to work with a group of students, using another teaching method such as interactive writing or interactive editing. The opportunity to work one-to-one is also possible, using this model. The work done by the special teacher should be additional rather than replacement. The students could participate in guided reading twice, once with the classroom teacher, and once with the special teacher.

A collaboration of this kind is based on the assumption that services provided using an in-class model can be more effective than those that pull a student out of the

classroom. It also assumes that aligning teaching methods used with students in special education and remedial reading benefits the student. Classroom teachers and special teachers should use the same teaching methods. The value of student familiarity with teaching methods and expectations shared by special teachers and the classroom teacher cannot be underestimated. Many of the students who are struggling or are placed in special education are those who are most confused by classroom routines. The use of an in-class collaboration and the alignment of teaching methods is an effective inclusion model.

## Prompting for Problem Solving

During guided reading the teacher listens to the students read. The teacher is looking for problems or confusions. The teacher observes the behaviors students use when they encounter difficulty. The teacher can choose to prompt the student at points of difficulty to help solve the problem. A prompt is a question that helps the student think about a way to solve the problem. A prompt becomes strategic or appropriately focused when it is made to support what the student is trying to do. For example, if a student is reading, "I went to the toy shop," and is unsure of the word *shop*, the teacher might provide the prompt, "What would make sense there?" In other words, the teacher asks the student to consider what was read and think about the meaning as a way to solve the problem. If there is confusion about the word *went*, the teacher might ask the student to look at the word and ask what is known about the word— perhaps the letters. The point of a prompt is to help the student use what is known to solve the problem rather than rely on the teacher to provide the answers. Since the goal is independent reading, the process of guided reading is one that encourages the use of independent problem solving behaviors.

A prompt is a question or suggestion from the teacher that focuses the students' attention on a way to solve confusions they are having as they read. A prompt is like a nudge in the right direction. The teacher gives a hint to where or how the problem might be solved, or what the student might do or think about to solve the problem. Prompts are used to problem solve an unknown word during reading. Prompts can direct a student's attention to a reading behavior or a source of information that might be used to solve a problem encountered in the text. Early reading behaviors such as directionality, reading each word, reading a line of text from left to right and then returning to the beginning of the following line, and reading top to bottom are generally taught during shared reading and interactive writing. Guided reading focuses on the practicing of behaviors and using various sources of information to problem solve as text is read.

Prompts during guided reading are questions that can be asked of students to help them think about using what they know to solve their own problems. Prompts about reading behaviors and prompts about sources of information can be used to encourage them to problem solve independently, not only during guided reading, but in other texts as well.

## Sources of Information

There are sources of information in texts that support student attempts to solve or correct a problem with text. One primary source of this information is the letter-sound relationship called phonics. What do the students know about letters and sounds that they can use to decode unknown words?

Understanding the vocabulary and following the meaning of the text represent the source of information we call comprehension. Does the student know the word? Can the student figure out the word, using a context clue? Does what the student read make any sense or have any meaning? Does the student monitor his or her own text comprehension during the reading? Students who monitor for comprehension know what they know. They also know what they don't know and try to figure it out. Students who comprehend the text can be expected to both answer questions and develop questions about the text. Practice of the behaviors used to develop comprehension is an important element of guided reading.

## Reading Behaviors

Good readers have particular behaviors they use when they attempt to read text. They have strategies they use to solve their problems. When they encounter a word they don't know, they usually stop and think about what they might know about the word. They might locate a known word in the text and use it to figure out the word. They might also look for parts of the word that can be used to figure it out. It could be a single letter, a combination of letters, or even an ending rime. Good readers monitor what they are reading, using phonics. They also use comprehension strategies to think about what they read and what it means. They try to read with more fluency to help comprehend what they read and to become more efficient in their reading.

Guided reading is used to assist students in developing necessary and strategic reading behaviors. They need to monitor their own reading behavior for accurate decoding and for comprehension. This monitoring is literally listening to themselves read and paying attention to both accuracy and meaning. They also need to learn to compare information from various sources. For example, does the word I read look like the word that is on the page? Or, does the word I read make any sense in this sentence or story? Fluent reading is an important feature of good reading behavior. Does the student read the text quickly and accurately, which means fluently, with phrasing and expression? This fluency contributes to comprehension because it allows the reader to focus on the meaning of the text instead of on decoding words. The most important reading behavior is correction. Correction occurs when the student is at a point of difficulty and attempts to use sources of information to solve the problem. The ability to correct is the hallmark of the proficient, independent reader.

Many teachers are too helpful when they listen to and support students during their reading. Teachers often give their students help, such as telling them a word, when they have information that they could use to solve their own problems. Teachers also frequently give a prompt that is too general and doesn't take into account what they know about the student's strengths and needs. Prompts that match what the student attempts or where the student is confused are effective ways to support and increase student independence in problem solving.

While we expect that students will be able to read almost everything they encounter in a guided reading selection, we also expect them to encounter different points of difficulty in a text and use individual means to solve the problem. Our goal is that the students are monitoring their reading in such a way that they are

### Sources of Information
Phonics
Comprehension

### Reading Behaviors
Monitoring
Comparing sources of information
Fluency
Correction

aware that their reading is either accurate or that they are at a point of difficulty and either know or don't know what to do to solve the problem they have encountered. Once a student has made a prediction, sources of information can be compared until the information predicted is either confirmed or discounted. **This is when the teacher provides a prompt: when a student has been unsuccessful in using what he or she knows.** The teacher's role in guided reading will always vary, depending on the success of the problem solving done by individual students in the group.

The teacher might suggest using a specific strategy or ask a question of the student to help him determine what he can do by himself to solve the problem. The goal is always to help students become more independent readers and to suggest behaviors that they can use in any reading situation, not just solving this problem, but being able to solve another problem on another day in another text with more ease.

## Prompts to Use During Guided Reading

### Sources of Information

**Phonics**
*Could you look at the letters of the word and see if you know a word that begins (or ends) like that?*

*Does what you read look that way?*

*What do you know about this word?*

*Do you see a part you know?*

**Comprehension**
*Could you listen to what you've read so far and try a word that makes sense there?*

*Does the word you read make sense in this text?*

*What has the author told you so far?*

### Reading Behaviors

**Monitoring**
*Do you see a word you know?*
*Does it help you?*

*Does what you read match the text?*

*You stopped. What are you thinking about?*

*Can you read that again and listen to how it sounds?*

**Comparing Sources of Information**
*Is there anything you know about the text that helps you with this word?*

*Can you compare this (the word you tried that made sense) and this (the letters you would see if it were that word) to help you?*

**Fluency**
*Can you read this again, only quicker (and/or with expression)?*

*Can you try to read this the way you speak?*

**Correction**
*Good try. Do you think that works here?*

*What can you do to help yourself solve this problem?*

*You said_____. Could it be_____?*
*Did you check_____?*

## Practice Your Prompt Activity

### What prompt would you select for each example?

- The text reads, "Yesterday, I went to the park." The student reads, "Yesterday, I goed to the park."

- The text reads, "The earth rotates on its axis." The student reads, "The earth rolls on its axis," but then pauses and appears to be thinking.

- The text reads, "My husband is very tired, and is in desperate need of a good night's rest." The student reads, "My husband is very tired, and is in deputy need of a good night's rest."

- The text reads, "Baby Bear looked in the toy shop window." The student reads, "Baby Bear looked in the toy store window."

- The text reads, "Once upon a time, three bears lived in a house by the woods." The student reads, "Once upon a time, three bears lived in a house by the forest, no, woods."

- The text reads, "We are going to stay at Grandma's house tonight." The student reads, "We are going to..." and stops. (The teacher knows that the student knows the words *play* and *stop*.)

- The text reads, "I love my new puppy." The student reads, "I love my new dog."

## After Guided Reading

The time spent after guided reading is important for enjoyment and understanding of the text. Reading as a pleasurable activity is an attitude that should be modeled by the teacher. **Our goal is not just to have students who can read; we also want students who want to read.** This time is also used to have a discussion about the text read during guided reading. Comprehension probes are a useful way to ensure that the students have read with understanding and that they comprehend the major points of the story. It is also common to make one or two teaching points at the end of the reading. Unlike the teaching points made *during* the guided reading that are individual in nature, the teaching points *after* the guided reading usually focus on something that will be of benefit to the whole group.

## Discussion

The discussion that takes place at the end of the reading is designed to help students think about what they read. This post-reading discussion is an opportunity for them to share ideas, feelings, and personal interpretations of the text. What did they learn from the text? What are they still confused about? Did they enjoy the story? The discussion helps the teacher probe for comprehension. It is also during the discussion that we help students enjoy and understand what they have read.

If the text is a fictional piece, the teacher may begin by asking the students to simply clarify the events of the story. As the students work together to give a simple retelling, they are encouraged to listen to each other's interpretations and either agree or disagree. In case of disagreement, the students are prompted to return to the text to clarify misunderstandings. The teacher can help them include the important parts of the story and use proper sequence and specific language. As a participant of the discussion, the teacher is also able to prompt the students to deeper understanding by asking questions that require higher level thinking skills. During the introduction, the students may have made predictions about the content of the text or the outcome of the story. During the post-reading discussion, they have the opportunity to check their initial predictions against the actual content of the text. Some stories require them to use inference in order to understand the text. Teachers can ensure that the students have not missed important information that was implied but not directly stated by asking appropriate questions and listening to the students' responses. If the text was a nonfiction piece, the discussion might focus on unfamiliar vocabulary and content that is new to the students. The teacher can use comprehension probes to ensure that the students have a good understanding of the text. They can be asked to answer questions and then form their own questions as part of the post-reading discussion. The discussion can help determine if they are monitoring their text comprehension.

> ### After Guided Reading
>
> Talk about the story to enhance understanding.
>
> Possibly return to the text for one or two teaching points.

The discussion should be conversational in tone and avoid the appearance of a quiz or test. The students should be actively encouraged to share what they know from reading the text, raise questions about the text, and make connections to their own lives and experiences. The discussion is critical to the ongoing success of guided reading. The students need to learn that reading is both enjoyable and useful. There are stories that can entertain, inform, and challenge the reader. Reading is a source of information and a necessary tool for life after school. Guided reading is a safe and supportive way for students to become better readers at both the skill level and the comprehension level.

Comprehension probes can be useful in stimulating and guiding the discussion after the guided reading. A probe is a question you ask to clarify a student's comprehension after the reading.

> ### Probes for Comprehension
>
> Did this story end the way you thought it would? How was it different?
>
> Can you retell what you read in your own words?
>
> What questions do you still have about this text?
>
> What did you learn from this text?
>
> What might you have done if you were a character in this text?
>
> Did this text remind you of something that has happened to you or someone you know?

## Teaching Points

Individual teaching points are usually made *during* the guided reading and to an individual student at the point of difficulty. Teaching points made *after* the guided reading focus on all of the students in the group. Throughout the reading, the teacher observes reading behaviors and notates potential teaching points. Once all the students in the group have completed the reading of the text, the teacher may choose to return to the text for one or two teaching points. Teaching points are most powerful when they come from the experiences of students during the reading. Teachers may anticipate a need for a teaching point, based on prior experiences with the students. If, however, the students do not demonstrate a need for assistance during the reading, there is no need to address that particular teaching point after the lesson. If no common teaching point is identified during the reading, the guided reading lesson can conclude after the discussion.  Students will have the opportunity to read these books again during independent reading.

# Possible Teaching Points for Guided Reading

These teaching points can be addressed using guided reading from both fiction and nonfiction texts.

## Alphabetic Principle
Letter recognition

Letter-name correspondence

Letter-sound correspondence

Alphabetic order

## Reading Behaviors
Monitor for phonics and comprehension

Compare sources of information for problem solving

Fluency

Correction

## Phonemic Awareness and Phonics
Hear sounds in words

Inflectional endings

Rhyming

Syllabication

Compound words

Onset and rime

Segmentation

Chunking and blending

Root words

Sounds in sequence

Analogies

High frequency words

Spelling patterns

Consonants, blends, short and long vowels, digraphs, diphthongs

Alliteration

Suffixes, prefixes, root words, derivations, and word origins

## Language Structure
Punctuation and capitalization

Spelling and word analysis

Sentence structure

Grammar

Vocabulary and word choice

Parts of speech

Word usage

Irregular words

Contractions

Antonyms, synonyms, homographs, homophones

Metaphors, similes, idioms

## Text Comprehension

### Structural Features of Informational Materials
Locate the title, table of contents, author, illustrator, chapter headings, glossaries, and indexes

Outlining and graphic organizers

Paragraph development

Interpretation of diagrams, charts, and graphs

Sequence, chronological order

Compare, contrast persuasive text

Determine cause and effect

Distinguish fact from opinion

### Structural Features of Literary Materials
Distinguish common forms of literature, such as poetry, drama, fiction and nonfiction, fantasies, fables, myths, legends, and fairy tales

Know strategies of reading for different purposes

Determine sequence, figurative language, word choice, sentence structure, line length, punctuation, rhythm, rhyme, and repetition

## Analysis of Text Features
Use pictures and context to determine unknown words and make predictions

Confirm or discount predictions in order to make new predictions or modify predictions

Respond to *who, what, where, when,* and *how* questions

Follow written directions (one step, two step, multiple steps, etc.)

Confirm predictions by identifying key words

Ask clarifying questions

Restate facts and details

Recognize and explain cause and effect

Connect the text to life experiences

Relate prior knowledge to the text

Retell familiar stories, expository, narrative passages

Make inferences

Know essential elements of text

Distinguish the main idea from supporting details

## Narrative Analysis
Distinguish fantasy from reality

Identify plot, character, setting, and important events

Determine the underlying theme or moral in a selected text

Identify beginning, middle, and end

Understand the author's purpose

Compare and contrast elements presented by different authors

Identify the speaker and recognize the difference between first and third person narration

**lit•er•a•cy  cen•ter**  \lĭt´ər-ə-sē sĕn´tər\

1: Independent tasks or activities that reinforce classroom learning and require no teacher assistance.

2: A powerful way to support literacy learning.

# 4. Introduction to Literacy Centers

## Literacy Centers Defined

Literacy centers provide meaningful activities that students are able to complete without teacher assistance. Centers are designed to be supportive of the rest of the learning that is going on in the classroom. Rather than an activity that emphasizes new learning, literacy centers allow students to practice and increase proficiency on previous learning. The keys to successful literacy centers are students who know the purpose of the center, students who know their job while in the center, and tasks in the center on which they can be independent. Independent work can be individual work or work that is accessible with the support of a peer.

Literacy centers should be considered centers of activity rather than specific places in a classroom. A center might be a plastic tub of materials, a plastic bag, an individual student's desktop, or even a space on the floor. Students might work alone in some centers and in small groups in other centers. A center might be as simple as an opportunity to read or write independently or as active as a center for book making.

## Purposes of Literacy Centers

Literacy centers give students an opportunity to independently practice reading, writing, listening, and speaking skills in a supportive environment. They allow the teacher time and opportunity to work with individual students or small groups of students. Literacy centers allow flexible grouping where the teacher can organize groups of students to work together for various reasons. The groups might focus on skills practice in one center and on comprehension in another.

Literacy centers are process-oriented tasks. It is not necessarily the product that the students create that is of primary interest. Literacy centers also allow them to make choices as to the type of activities they select to support their learning. Positive experiences encourage them to become more independent learners.

One primary purpose of literacy centers is to give the teacher the opportunity to focus uninterrupted attention on guided reading groups. With all of the students in the classroom occupied with meaningful, independent tasks, the teacher can convene reading groups and provide individual attention to support reading. This model is considered an intervention that can be delivered in a classroom by an individual teacher without the support of a reading specialist, special education teacher, or instructional aide.

### Values of Literacy Centers

Allow the teacher to focus on guided reading

Encourage students to be independent

Contribute to effective classroom management

Provide positive opportunities to practice

## Organization

The environment of the classroom is important to the success of literacy centers. It is important in guided reading that the teacher is able to give concentrated and uninterrupted attention to the reading group. To do this, appropriate routines have to be established for the rest of the class and their participation in various literacy centers.

One might say that you are ready to begin guided reading when you are able to send all of your students to literacy centers, sit in the middle of your classroom, and have no students approach you with questions or problems. This represents students who understand their jobs in literacy centers, understand what is expected of them, and understand how to proceed independently. To accomplish this, it takes specific training by the teacher for each student in each literacy center in which they will participate.

Each student should be able to work independently in each literacy center. Centers that call for group work have the added requirement that students understand how they are expected to work in the group. It is important because guided reading lessons are usually short sessions (ten to fifteen minutes) and very strategic in their design and focus. It is difficult to maintain that focus if other students in the classroom are interrupting or asking for help with their work in a literacy center. Remember that literacy centers are designed at an independent level with tasks the students understand. One of the major obstacles to guided reading is a literacy center where the procedures and expectations are not completely understood by the students.

## Establishing Routines

Introduce a center by going over the rules and procedures that apply to the center. This should include what materials are to be used, where they are stored, how to get them and arrange them, and how to put them away correctly. Have groups of students practice these centers while the teacher observes and makes notes of any problems. This information should be used to revise procedures to increase the efficiency of the center.

On subsequent days, introduce new centers with the same thorough explanation of routines and procedures. Again, the teacher should observe and note any changes that are necessary for the smooth operation of the center. These procedures should be continued until there are enough centers to include all of the students in either independent or small group work.

### Students Need to Know

Where do I get the supplies I need?

What is my job in this center?

Where do I put things when I am finished?

Is there a signal to change activities?

These centers should be allowed to run for a number of days so that they can be evaluated. They should be allowed to operate without any intervention or assistance from the teacher. When the students no longer approach the teacher for guidance or to ask questions, guided reading groups can be convened.

Students need to be instructed not to interrupt during the guided reading session. They should be told to hold any questions or problems until the guided reading is completed. Between guided reading groups, the teacher should move around the classroom, check the operation of each center, and provide any support that might be needed. The students might remain in their center when the next guided reading group is convened; this is also a good time for them to change centers. Some teachers use a schedule of rotation, while others allow student choice of centers. Still others use a combination of rotation and choice.

Not all literacy centers will last for the entire school year. Some will lose the students' interest and will need to be revised. Others might need to be discontinued entirely. As new learning is developed in the classroom, new literacy centers will need to be developed to support student practice on this learning.

Literacy centers are an important part of every classroom. The importance of practice cannot be overestimated as a method to support student independence. Literacy centers are also a singular opportunity for providing necessary intervention in a classroom. The individual attention that can be provided in small group work is made possible by effective and efficient literacy centers.

## Questions to Ask about Organization

Are the centers at the students' independent level?

Are the center activities ones that the students enjoy?

Are the students able to choose a center?

Are all centers literacy focused?

Do the students need more instruction in a center?

Are all of the routines and expectations clear?

# 5. Literacy Centers You Can Use

# 1. Retell

## Goal

The students will read a variety of texts and be able to retell the major events or information accurately.

## Basic Center

### Materials

A variety of texts from read alouds, shared reading, guided reading, or interactive writing

### Preparation

The teacher will:

- Provide a variety of texts (read alouds, shared readings, guided readings, interactively written texts).

- Organize the texts so that the students can easily access them.

- Model procedures for retelling during whole and small group instruction.

- Provide opportunities for the students to participate in retellings and receive feedback.

### Procedures

The students will:

- Read a selected text, either alone or with a partner.

- Retell key events or important information from the text to another person orally.

## Beyond the Basic Center

### Additional Center Ideas

- Provide the students with flannel boards and flannel pieces that correspond to favorite stories that have been read aloud. The students work alone or with a partner to manipulate the pieces as they retell the important events of the story.

- Provide the students with texts from prior guided reading lessons. They then use a piece of paper that has been divided into four sections and illustrate key points of the texts. The students use their illustrations to help them as they orally retell the new information to one another.

**Students reading a variety of texts.**

- Provide the students with a variety of art media (crayons, markers, paint, glitter, sticks) to create props, settings, or characters from the text. They use the materials they create to retell the important information to a small audience of their peers. The students may work on this project alone or with a partner.

- After reading a story the students record their retelling using a tape recorder. They then listen to their retelling and use a rubric to assess their performance.

- After reading expository text, the students create a graphic organizer that displays key information. The students can then use this graphic organizer to retell what they have learned in an oral presentation.

### Additional Resources

Brown, M. *Four Fur Feet*. Disney Press, 1999. ISBN 078680422X

Edwards, P. *Four Famished Foxes and Fosdyke*. HarperCollins Children's Books, 1997. ISBN 006443480X

Edwards, P. *Some Smug Slug*. HarperCollins Children's Books, 1999. ISBN 0060247924

Kuskin, K. *Roar and More*. Harcourt Brace & Company, 1990. ISBN 0064430197

Martin, B., & Archambault, J. *Chicka, Chicka Boom Boom*. Aladdin Paperbacks, 2000. ISBN 068983568X

Students prepare to tape record their reading.

Retelling a favorite story using a flannel board.

Reading together is fun.

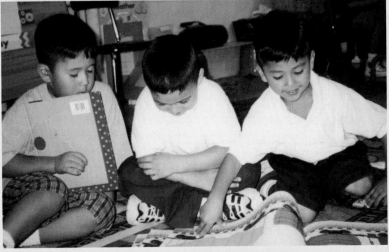

# 2. Overhead

## Goal

The students will practice phonemic awareness activities to notice, think about, and work with sounds in spoken language.

## Basic Center

### Materials

Overhead projector
Overhead transparencies
Various pictures or photographs

### Preparation

The teacher will:

- Find pictures that have many items to label (magazine clippings, workbook pages, photographs).

- Duplicate pictures onto overhead transparencies.

- Organize the transparencies into folders, sheet protectors, or binders.

- Locate an accessible area of the classroom to place the overhead in order to project the image.

- Instruct, model, and practice with the students how to operate the overhead projector.

- Demonstrate for the students how to isolate, identify, or segment phonemes using overhead pictures.

### Procedures

The students will:

- Choose pictures from folders, sheet protectors, or binders to place on the overhead projector.

- Practice a variety of phonemic skills at the overhead center.

## Beyond the Basic Center

### Additional Center Ideas

- Make overhead pictures of the students in your class. Teach them to substitute one phoneme for another to make a new name. Demonstrate how to orally chant the names with a partner (*Linda, Binda, Cinda, Minda*).

- Devise a game to practice phoneme categorization called "Odd Sound OUT!" Use old workbook pictures or computer clip art to make overhead transparencies that have six to nine pictures per page. Cut the

**Using the overhead to practice a variety of phonemic skills.**

pictures apart and put them in a file box or baggie. The students play this game in pairs. One student chooses four pictures from the box or baggie, three of which have the same beginning sound and one that does not. The student lays the pictures on the overhead and says the name (bear, banana, cat, ball). The other student must tell which picture is the "Odd Sound OUT!"

- The teacher records many words in which the phonemes have been separated (/c/ /a/ /t/). The students listen to the sequence of separately spoken phonemes and combine the phonemes to form a word. Provide pictures representing the recorded words. The students find the corresponding picture, place it on the overhead, and blend the phonemes to say the word. Note: This center can use the same pictures to segment phonemes. The students put a picture on the overhead, say the name of the picture, segment the phonemes, and count the number of sounds in the word. Next, they place the correct number of unifix cubes or counters on the overhead under the picture.

- Using overhead pictures from content area studies, the students sort the pictures according to the number of syllables.

- Prepare transparencies with nursery rhyme pictures. The students select an overhead and recite the nursery rhyme.

### Additional Resources

Marzollo, J. *I Spy Spooky Night: A Book of Pictures in Riddles.* Scholastic Inc., 1996. ISBN 0590481371

Marzollo, J. *I Spy Treasure Hunt.* Scholastic, Inc., 1999. ISBN 0439042445

Marzollo, J. *I Spy: Year-Round Challenge.* Scholastic, Inc., 2001. ISBN 0439316340

Moroney, T. *A Classic Treasury of Nursery Songs & Rhymes.* Barnes & Noble Books, 2001. ISBN 076072380X

Opie, I. *Here Comes Mother Goose.* Candlewick Press, 1999. ISBN 0763606839

Stevens, J., & Crummel, S. *And the Dish Ran Away With the Spoon.* Harcourt, 2001. ISBN 0152022988

Taback, S. *This is the House That Jack Built.* Penguin Publishers, 2002. ISBN 0399234888

Yolen, J. *How Do Dinosaurs Say Goodnight?* Scholastic, Inc., 2000. ISBN 0590316818

**Listening for phonemes.**

**Reading and sorting words by syllables.**

**Reciting familiar nursery rhymes.**

# 3. Word Study

## Goal

The students will practice and apply their knowledge of phonics as they read words from sentences and text.

## Basic Center

### Materials

Word cards (high frequency, colors, numbers, content area words)

Container

Pocket chart

### Preparation

The teacher will:

- Purposely select familiar words from interactive writing, interactive editing, and shared reading texts that can be categorized according to meaning.

- Demonstrate, using the pocket chart and a group of word cards, how to read and sort cards into categories.

- Read the word cards one at a time and think aloud the reasoning for categorizing each word.

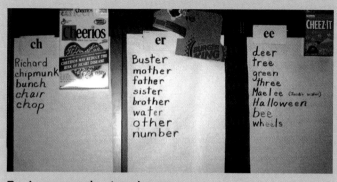

Environmental print charts.

## Procedures

The students will:

- Work with a partner to read and sort words by category.

- Share read the finished sort to verify placement of words in categories.

## Beyond the Basic Center

### Additional Center Ideas

- Collect a variety of pictures (workbook, clip art, magazine) and place them in a baggie. Prepare word cards with the phonic category (beginning sounds, ending sounds, vowel sounds) in order to sort the pictures. The students choose pictures and sort them by similar sound into appropriate categories.

- Collect examples or photographs of environmental print and display them on chart paper. Select one common spelling pattern from each example and label each chart. The students record and list other words with the same spelling pattern on the environmental charts. The students reread the charts with a partner.

- Create a "High Five" card game by duplicating game cards (see Page 145). Write one word on each card that has a common rime (*cat, bat, fat, flat*). The students play in pairs. Each player receives six cards. The object is to form groups of five words with the same rime. Additional cards are stacked in the middle as a draw pile. Using the cards dealt, Player 1 asks, "Do you have a word that rhymes with *cat*?" Player 2

Using a pocket chart to sort words by category.

must silently read his or her cards and either give one rhyming card to Player 1 or tell the player to "High Five" and draw an additional card from the pile. The players alternate turns. When five rimes are collected in a player's hand, the player lays the cards down and reads the rime family. Play continues until one player has no cards left. The winner is determined by whoever has the most groups of rimes laid down.

- Prepare word cards with contractions and the words that form the contraction. The students read and sort the cards, matching the contraction to its word parts. A variation could include other parts of speech, such as synonyms, antonyms, homophones, or homographs.

- Using the game board template (see Page 146), duplicate and glue it into a file folder. Prepare the game board by writing one abbreviation/shortened word (*Dr., Ave., memo, ad*) in each space. Prepare game cards by writing the non-abbreviated/full word (*Doctor, Avenue, memorandum, advertisement*). The students play in pairs. Each student chooses a game piece to begin. Players alternate by drawing a card from the pile and reading the non-abbreviated/full word and then moving their game piece to the matching abbreviation/shortened word on the game board. This is a continuous game that lasts as long as there are cards in the pile to draw, read, and match.

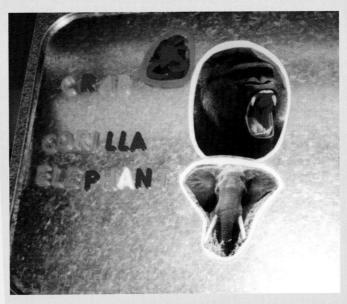

**Matching words to pictures.**

## Additional Resources

Cleary, B. *A Mink, a Fink, a Skating Rink.* Lerner Publishing Group, 2000. ISBN 1575054175

Cleary, B. *Under, Over, by the Clover: What is a Preposition?* Lerner Publishing Group, 2002. ISBN 1575055244

Heling, K. *Mouse Makes Words.* Random House Books for Young Readers, 2002. ISBN 0375813993

Heller, R. *Kites Sail High: A Book About Verbs.* Econo-Clad Books, 1998. ISBN 0833550255

Marzollo, J. *I Spy Little Letters.* Scholastic, Inc., 2000. ISBN 0439114969

McBrath, B. *The M&M's Brand Counting Book.* Charlesbridge Publishing, Inc., 1994. ISBN 0881068535

McCall, F. *A Huge Hog is a Big Pig.* HarperCollins Children's Books, 2002. ISBN 0060297654

McGrath, W. *The Cheerios Counting Book.* Scholastic, Inc., 1998. ISBN 0590683578

Wilbur, R. *The Disappearing Alphabet.* Harcourt, Inc., 2001. ISBN 015216362X

**Practicing beginning sounds.**

## Phonics

# 4. Skills Practice

### Goal
The students will read a variety of texts to practice skills in context.

### Basic Center

#### Materials
Tongue depressors labeled with grade-appropriate words (names, high frequency words, content words, bank words)

Jars or cans labeled with numbers 1 through 5

Counting Syllables recording sheet (optional—see Page 147)

#### Preparation
The teacher will:

- Write grade appropriate words/pictures on tongue depressors.

- Choose words from shared readings and interactive writings. Model how to determine the number of syllables in each word by clapping.

#### Procedures
The students will:

- Select tongue depressors and read words/pictures.

- Determine the number of syllables by clapping.

- Sort words by number of syllables into labeled jars or cans.

- Read words in each jar to a classmate.

- List words and number of syllables on the Counting Syllables recording sheet, if appropriate.

Alphabet soup.

### Beyond the Basic Center

#### Additional Center Ideas

- Create an "Alphabet Soup" center by filling a large bowl with many magnetic letters. The students use a ladle to scoop out a serving of letters into a plastic bowl. The letters are sorted and named.

- Provide the students with a phonic pattern and magnetic letters. Make task cards featuring the phonic pattern as well as several example words. The students use magnetic letters to create as many words as possible using the designated pattern.

- The students create a page for a class book using alliteration based on the first letter of their name (Kind Karen kisses kooky kangaroos in Kenya.). Compile the pages into a book and place it in the class library for independent reading.

- Create a class bulletin board with flowers and their roots. The root word is written on the root of the plant. The new words are written on the petals and leaves of the flowers. The students add to the board by thinking of a different root word and making a flower (*friend - friends, friendly, friendless*). Provide the necessary materials.

- Make a large tree out of paper and attach it to the classroom wall. During interactive writing negotiate class definitions for various parts of speech. Select several die cuts that represent those parts of speech

Students sort words by number of syllables.

(pears-homophones, leaves-nouns, birds-verbs, butterflies-adjectives, ants-antonyms). The students read the definitions and the existing tree examples. The students write new words on appropriate die cuts and attach them to the tree. Then they reread all the words.

## Additional Resources

Clements, A. *DOUBLE TROUBLE in Walla Walla.* Millbrook Press, 1997. ISBN 0761302751

Estes, K. *The Silly AB Seas.* Greene Bark Press, 1997. ISBN 188085127X

Heller, R. *Many Luscious Lollipops: A Book about Adjectives.* Putnam Publishing Group, 1991. ISBN 0448031515

Heller, R. *Kites Sail High: A Book about Verbs.* Putnam Publishing Group, 1998. ISBN 0689112896

Trelease, J., & Prelutsky, J. *Read Aloud Rhymes for the Very Young.* Alfred A. Knopf, 1986. ISBN 0394872185

Walton, R. *So Many Bunnies: A Bedtime ABC and Counting Book.* Lathrop, Lee & Shepard Books, 1998. ISBN 0688136575

Parts of speech tree.

A class alliteration book.

Root word bulletin board.

A root word is the main word from which other words are created.

# 5. Strategy

## Goal
The students will apply their knowledge of letters and sounds to problem solve unknown words.

## Basic Center

### Materials
Familiar shared reading texts written on large charts

Replacement word cards organized in labeled envelopes

Paper clips

### Preparation
The teacher will:

- Choose a familiar shared reading chart with words that can easily and meaningfully be replaced (Humpty Dumpty sat on a *wall (chair, stool, bed)*.

- Make the word cards (*chair, stool, bed*) the same size as the word to be replaced. On the back of each card, place a picture that corresponds to the word.

- Cut a slit over the word to be replaced and insert a paper clip for the word card.

- Demonstrate how to manipulate cards and problem solve new words during shared reading, using different sources of information.

Using a pocket chart.

## Procedures
The students will:

- Read a familiar shared reading chart.

- Choose a word card and slip a new word under the paper clip.

- Reread the text, problem solving the new word.

## Beyond the Basic Center

### Additional Center Ideas

- Determine a phonic pattern (blends, digraphs, diphthongs) that the students need to use when solving new words. Using familiar texts, the students locate and highlight (marker, removable tape, Wikki Stix) words that exhibit the pattern.

- Use a familiar shared reading text with separate corresponding pictures. Display the sentences in a pocket chart. The students reread the selection and match the pictures to the appropriate sentences.

Rereading and manipulating familiar shared reading pieces.

- Rewrite a familiar shared reading text on a chart, leaving spaces where words have been omitted. Prepare separate cards with the omitted words. The students read one sentence at a time. Using multiple sources of information, they locate and replace the missing words. The students reread the entire text to a partner for problem solving and accuracy.

- During the year, add words to the word wall containing common rimes (-ay, -ill, -ake). Highlight these rimes and demonstrate how parts of words help to solve new words. The students choose a text from class interactive writings and shared readings. They search for words that contain rimes, using the word wall as a resource. The students record the word sound and the word(s) they used from the word wall and highlight the rimes using yellow markers.

- Provide a collection of familiar shared reading texts. In pairs, the students identify and highlight key words. The students brainstorm a list of synonyms for the highlighted words. They reread each sentence, substituting synonyms and checking for meaning.

## Additional Resources

Bloom, B. *WOLF!* Orchard Books, 1999. ISBN 0531301559

DeGross, M. *Donovan's Word Jar.* HarperCollins Publishing, 1998. ISBN 0064420892

Parish, P. *Key to the Treasure.* Bantam Doubleday Dell Books for Young Readers, 1980. ISBN 0440444381

Price, R. *Night of the Living Mad Libs.* Putnam & Grossett Publishing Group, 1995. ISBN 0843137355

Priddy, R. *My Big Word Book.* St. Martin's Press, 2002. ISBN 0312490755

Ringgold, F. *Cassie's Word Quilt.* Random House Children's Books, 2002. ISBN 0375812008

Westley, J. *Rime Time: Building Word Families with Letter Tiles.* Primary Concepts/Concepts to Go, 1999. ISBN 1893791009

Locating phonic patterns.

# 6. Interactive Charts

## Goal
The students will manipulate sections of familiar readings in order to practice reading fluently.

## Basic Center

### Materials
Sentence strips

Pocket chart

Container, envelope, or baggie

Copies of text

### Preparation
The teacher will:

- Choose familiar shared reading pieces that have words or phrases that can be easily modified.

- Write texts of shared reading on sentence strips and display them in a pocket chart.

- Choose words and phrases to be modified and write alternate choices. Store these in a container, envelope, or baggie near the pocket chart.

- Highlight the portion of text to be changed in some way.

### Procedures
The students will:

- Read the text in its original format, either alone or with a friend.

Jack and Jill

went up the hill,

To fetch a pail of

water.

Jack fell down,

and broke his crown,

And Jill came

tumbling after!

**An interactive nursery rhyme.**

- Replace portions of the original text with the choices provided.

- Reread the new text fluently.

- Repeat this procedure, using multiple text choices.

## Beyond the Basic Center

### Additional Center Ideas

- Use common chants or nursery rhymes, allowing the students to replace character names with their own names or the names of their classmates.

- Rewrite familiar text from shared reading or interactive writing on sentence strips. Cut the text apart into word units. The students then rebuild the text in the pocket chart, reading each word as it is added to the text. Once the text is completed, the students reread it fluently.

**Students play with letters to reread an interactive chart.**

- Use a shared reading or interactive writing text that is written in narrative or expository form. Sentences should extend beyond one line of print, providing return sweep possibilities. As part of a shared reading lesson, read the text fluently and determine the appropriate phrase units. Together, cut the passage apart by phrases. The students then rebuild the passage and reread the entire text fluently.

- Use a familiar piece of text that has examples of noun and pronoun agreement. Provide options for text change that would require the students to change the pronoun in order to maintain correct grammar. Reread the changed text fluently.

- Provide the students with examples of familiar text in which meaning can change, based on punctuation or emphasis. ("Sue, the nurse can't come right now," or, "Sue, the nurse, can't come right now.") The students work in pairs to manipulate punctuation and read the new text fluently.

### Additional Resources

Dahl, R. *Roald Dahl's Revolting Rhymes.* Penguin Putnam Books for Young Readers, 1995. ISBN 0140375333

Knowles, S. *Edward the Emu.* HarperCollins Publishers, 1998. ISBN 0064434990

Manning, J. *Who Stole the Cookies from the Cookie Jar?* HarperCollins Children's Books, 2001. ISBN 0694015156

Mayo, M. *Wiggle Waggle Fun: Stories and Rhymes for the Very Young.* Alfred A. Knopf, 2002. ISBN 0375815295

Wood, D. *The Little Mouse, the Red Ripe Strawberry, and the Hungry Bear.* Child's Play of England, 1989. ISBN 0859531821

Rebuilding text.

Teacher instructing students on center procedures.

# 7. Listening and Speaking

## Goal

The students will listen and respond to various texts in order to improve fluency and comprehension.

## Basic Center

### Materials

Tape recorders with earphones

Books or other texts stored in bags or other containers

Audiotapes of the books or texts

Blank paper or response sheets (optional)

Writing tools

### Preparation

The teacher will:

- Designate an area in the room where the tape recorder and materials will be located. Organize the materials so that they will be easily accessible to the students.

- Teach the students procedures for working at the center, including how to operate the tape recorder.

### Procedures

The students will:

- Follow the established procedures and listen to the texts on tape.

- Respond to the story orally or in written format, using prompts provided by the teacher. (Did you like the story? Why? What is your favorite part of the story? Why? What personal connections did you make to the text? What do you think is the most important idea expressed by the author? Why?)

## Beyond the Basic Center

### Additional Center Ideas

- Choose texts that contain many known and high frequency words. Record the text, pausing at the end of each sentence. The students listen to the tape and echo the reading, imitating your phrasing, expression, and intonation.

- Record multiple-step directions related to a content area. The students listen to the directions in order to create a simple project (recipe, art project, science experiment).

- Provide a blank audiotape for each student. The students practice reading a familiar text several times and then record their reading. They listen to the tapes and self-assess their reading using a fluency rubric or scale.

- You or the students record brief phone messages. The students listen and write the message on a phone memo (see Page 148).

Listening to texts on tape.

Following multiple step directions.

Practicing for fluent reading.

- Model questioning during read alouds. Next, a small group of students listens to a recorded text and asks each other questions about the text. Then the students record the questions on paper for other groups to think about as they listen to the text.

### Additional Resources

Carfi, J. *Greatest Answering Machine Messages of All Time.* CCC Publications, 1993. ISBN 0918259541

Curtis, J. *Today I Feel Silly & Other Moods That Make My Day.* HarperCollins Publishers, 1998. ISBN 0060245603

De Capua, S. *We Need Directions!* Scholastic, Inc., 2001. ISBN 0516273809

Egan, V. *1001 Questions & Answers: World of Knowledge.* Barnes & Noble Books, 1997. ISBN 0760704104

Leokum, A. *The Big Book of Tell Me Why: 3 Volumes in 1.* Barnes & Noble Books, 1990. ISBN 0880293179

Myers, S. *WINGS.* Scholastic, Inc., 2000. ISBN 0590033778

Stevens, J. and Crummel, S. *Cook-A-Doodle-Doo!.* Harcourt, 1999. ISBN 0152019243

Individual tapes for students.

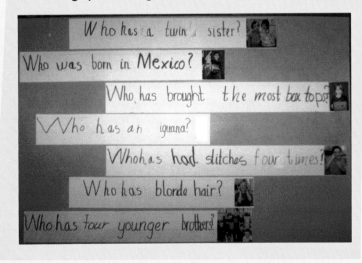

Modeling questioning.

Who has a twin sister?
Who was born in Mexico?
Who has brought the most box tops?
Who has an iguana?
Who has had stitches four times?
Who has blonde hair?
Who has four younger brothers?

# 8. Familiar Reading

## Goal
The students will practice orally rereading text to improve word recognition and fluency.

## Basic Center

### Materials
Selection of familiar texts

Storage container(s)

### Preparation
The teacher will:

- Collect texts that the students have used and are familiar with from read aloud, shared reading, or guided reading lessons.

- Organize the texts so the students can choose a book they are capable of reading.

- Teach the students how to choose appropriate books for familiar rereading.

- Demonstrate, model, and practice how to read to a partner and provide feedback.

### Procedures
The students will:

- Choose a familiar book.

- Read their chosen book to a partner.

- Listen to encouragement and feedback from their partner regarding the reading.

## Beyond the Basic Center

### Additional Center Ideas
- Create a "Read the Room" center by collecting reading pointers and placing them in a container. With a partner or small group, the students read familiar text that is displayed in the room. The text may be interactive writing or shared reading.

- Collect or prepare familiar books on tape, provide a tape recorder and individual headphones to create a tape-assisted reading center. The students read aloud simultaneously or as an echo with the taped model.

- Prepare reader's theater scripts based on familiar texts that are rich in dialogue. The students choose roles, rehearse dialogue, and interact with peers as they prepare a performance for their classmates.

**Reading together to improve fluency.**

- Discuss aspects of fluency with the students. Interactively create a fluency rubric with the entire class. Model with the students how to use the rubric to provide specific feedback on each other's reading. Duplicate the rubric and place it with the containers of familiar texts. The students work with a partner to read aloud and assess fluency according to the rubric.

- The students choose a portion of text to practice reading aloud for speed and automaticity. They time their first reading by themselves or with a partner, using a stopwatch. The students record the text title and time on a fluency chart (see Page 152). On subsequent days, they will practice reading the same text and continue timing and recording. The students choose a new piece of text weekly.

### Additional Resources
Bany-Winters, L. *Show Time!: Music, Dance & Drama Activities for Kids.* Chicago Review Press Inc., 2000. ISBN 1556523610

Bauer, C. *Presenting Reader's Theatre: Plays and Poems to Read Aloud.* H. W. Wilson Company, 1987. ISBN 0824207483

Read the room.

Cronin, D. *Giggle, Giggle, Quack*. Simon & Schuster Books for Young Readers, 2002. ISBN 0689845065

Dahl, R. *Roald Dahl's Revolting Rhymes*. Alfred A. Knopf, 2002. ISBN 0375815562

Ehlert, L. *Waiting for Wings*. Harcourt, Inc., 2001. ISBN 0152026088

Hoberman, M. *You Read to Me, I'll Read to You! Very Short Stories to Read Together*. Little Brown Children's Books, 2001. ISBN 0316363502

Numeroff, L. *If You Take a Mouse to School*. HarperCollings Publishers, 2002. ISBN 0060283289

Palatini, M. *The Web Files*. Hyperion Books for Children, 2001. ISBN 078680419X

Tape-assisted reading center.

Timing reading for fluency.

# 9. Poetry

## Goal
The students will read familiar poetry to develop fluency, apply strategies, and practice skills in a meaningful way.

## Basic Center

### Materials
Poetry selections

Poetry books

Storage container

### Preparation
The teacher will:

- Collect copies of familiar poetry the class has read during shared reading. These selections could be formatted as large charts, class-made books, overhead transparencies, sentence strips in a pocket chart, or individual copies from an anthology.

- Organize and store the poetry selections in plastic bags, file folders, plastic tubs, cardboard boxes, or any convenient container.

### Procedures
The students will:

- Fluently read the poetry selections individually, in pairs or in small groups.

Organizing for the poetry center.

- Use the poetry selections to practice specific skills determined by the teacher (letter identification, high frequency words, descriptive language, prepositional phrases, metaphors).

- Locate examples of the specified skill.

## Beyond the Basic Center

### Additional Center Ideas
- Write poetry selections on sentence strips. The sentence strips could be cut apart by individual word, phrase, or stanza. The students sequence the poem by placing the sentence strips in a pocket chart and practice reading fluently.

- Label Popsicle sticks or tongue depressors with previously taught skills for the students to read and locate within the poetry selection (individual letters, rhyming words, punctuation, parts of speech, figurative language). The students may record their responses.

- Create a poetry cube by cutting off the top portion of two half-gallon milk cartons, leaving approximately six inches of carton. Insert the open ends of each carton (one inside the other) to form a cube. Cover the cube with contact paper and write poetry titles on each face. The students roll the cube to determine the poem they will locate, read, and use.

Choosing a poem to read.

- Provide the students with materials to create individual poetry books (construction paper, copies of poems, notebooks, art materials). The students can respond to these poems by illustrating, writing personal connections, or summarizing.

- The students cooperatively work to orally present a poetry selection. Oral presentations could include recitation, reader's theater, dramatic interpretations, choral reading, or audiotapes.

## Additional Resources

Asch, F., & Levin, T. *Cactus Poems*. Harcourt Brace & Company, 1998. ISBN 0152006761

Bunting, E. *MOONSTICK (The Seasons of the Sioux)*. HarperCollins Publishers, 1997. ISBN 0060248041

Greenberg, J. *Heart to Heart*. Harry N. Abrams, Inc., 2001. ISBN 0810943867

Holbrook, S. *Chicks Up Front*. Cleveland State University Poetry Center, 1998. ISBN 1880834391

Hopkins, L. *My America (A Poetry Atlas of the United States)*. Simon & Schuster Books for Young Readers, 2000. ISBN 0689812477

Katz, A. *Take Me Out of the Bathtub and Other Silly Dilly Songs*. Simon & Schuster Children's Publishing Division, 2001. ISBN 0689829035

Kay, V. *Tattered Sails*. G. P. Putnam's Sons, 2001. ISBN 0399233458

Sierra, J. *Antarctic Antics (A Book of Penguin Poems)*. Harcourt Brace & Company, 1998. ISBN 0152010068

Sierra, J. *Monster Goose*. Gulliver Books, Harcourt Inc., 2001. ISBN 0152020349

Weiss, G., & Thiele, B. *What A Wonderful World*. Simon & Schuster Children's Publishing Division, 1967. ISBN 0689800878

**Rebuilding poems in pocket charts.**

**Selecting familiar reading.**

Vocabulary

# 10. Dramatic Play

## Goal

The students will participate in dramatic interpretations to practice specialized vocabulary.

## Basic Center

### Materials

Puppets (commercial, student-made)

Presentation area (puppet theater, podium, table)

Vocabulary-rich text (books, scripts, poems, charts)

### Preparation

The teacher will:

- Choose texts for read aloud and shared reading that lend themselves to dramatic interpretation. The texts should include words or phrases that may be unfamiliar to the students. Engage the students in discussions to help them learn new words and concepts.

- Designate an area in the room where the drama center will be located.

- Organize the puppets and texts so they are easily accessible to the students.

- Teach the students procedures for performing at the center. Using a shared reading piece, model how to read text while acting it out.

- Model and discuss the role of an audience member.

## Procedures

The students will:

- Choose a text to practice reading and performing.

- Negotiate the reading responsibilities and select appropriate puppets.

- Read and act out the text, using proper intonation, expression, and fluency.

- Invite other classmates to watch the presentation.

## Beyond the Basic Center

### Additional Center Ideas

- Arrange texts of nursery rhymes, chants, or songs in plastic storage bags or tubs, along with appropriate props. The students chorally read the text and use props to act it out.

- Provide individual copies of scripts. The students determine the role they will read. The group of students practice reading the script in order to perform their interpretation.

- Establish a real-life simulation (bank, post office, news station, grocery store, restaurant, doctor's office, science laboratory) that would support a current unit of study. Gather specific materials and texts for the chosen simulation and determine a classroom location. As the students develop greater conceptual understandings from the unit of study, they add text and artwork to the simulation environment.

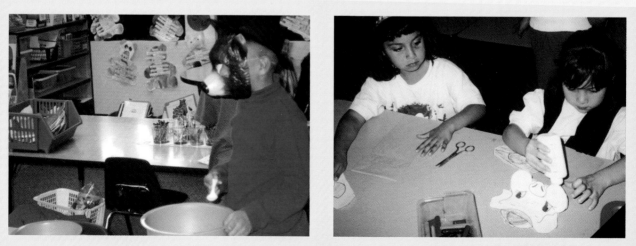

Preparing for a puppet show.

A variety of simulation drama centers.

- The students independently read a text of their choice. They choose a character, object, or animal from the reading in order to make a paper bag puppet. Then write a brief biographical summary using specific vocabulary from the reading. Using their puppet, the students put the character in the "spotlight" for a small group presentation.

- After a small group book discussion on fiction texts, the students take turns becoming a character in the book. Other students interview the "character" asking questions such as: Who is your favorite person? Who gives you the most problems? What is hard for you? The student answers questions in character, utilizing information from the book.

### Additional Resources

Cocca-Leffler, M. *Mr. Tanen's Ties*. Albert Whitman Publishers, 1999. ISBN 0807553018

Danziger, P. *Amber Brown Is Not a Crayon*. Scholastic Paperbacks, 1995. ISBN 059045899X

Frasier, D. *Miss Alaineus: A Vocabulary Disaster*. Harcourt, 2000. ISBN 0152021639

Greene, C. *At the Post Office*. Child's World, Incorporated, 1998. ISBN 1567664830

Oppel, F. *Why Do We Say It? (Stories Behind the Words, Expressions & Cliches We Use)*. Book Sales Inc., 1991. ISBN 1555210104

Poskanzer, S. *What's It Like To Be a Chef?* Troll Communications, 1990. ISBN 0816717982

Thistle, L. *Dramatizing Three Classic Tales*. Smith & Kraus Inc., 1999. ISBN 1575251922

Waters, K. *Samuel Eaton's Day: A Day in the Life of a Pilgrim Boy*. Scholastic, Inc., 1993. ISBN 059046311X

"Spotlight on Amber Brown!"

# 11. Vocabulary

## Goal

The students will read new words in context and use those words correctly in their oral and written language.

## Basic Center

### Materials

A variety of writing tools

9" x 12" construction paper

Word banks

Student dictionaries and thesauruses at a variety of levels

Large three-ring binder

### Preparation

The teacher will:

- Read aloud from a variety of texts that contain rich and varied vocabulary.

- Encourage discussion about unfamiliar words.

- Use interactive writing to create word banks for content area vocabulary and overused words (*barn, season, explorer, said, like, good*). Display the word banks and utilize them during direct instruction.

## Procedures

The students will:

- Choose a word from a word bank and write it clearly on a 9" x 12" sheet of construction paper.

**Ocean Creatures**

whale · sea turtle
scorpion fish · crab
stingray · seal
sea horse · squid
jellyfish · blowfish
rock fish · fish
hammerhead shark · porpoise
octopus · clam
shark · oyster
swordfish · pelican
dolphin · seagull
eel
sea anemone
starfish

**Rereading familiar vocabulary from shared reading pieces.**

- If needed, use dictionaries and thesauruses as a resource.

- Use pictures and/or sentences to clearly describe the meaning of the new word.

- Create illustrations that enhance the reader's understanding of the sentence(s).

- Add the completed sheet to a class binder and read the accumulated pages. Place the binder in the class library.

## Beyond the Basic Center

### Additional Center Ideas

- Collect many pictures representing the current content area of study. Place the pictures in an envelope. The students select pictures from the envelope and arrange them in order to tell a story. Use the content vocabulary from the pictures and orally share with a partner.

**A dictionary center focusing on vocabulary.**

Word banks for all seasons.

- Display the word bank that the class has created to accompany the current content area study. The students create crossword puzzles on graph paper, using the vocabulary words. Then they write their own definitions and clues. The students solve each other's crossword puzzles.

- Provide the students with individual word study notebooks or personal dictionaries. They add new vocabulary words found in their independent reading to their books. They add definitions, synonyms, sentences, or illustrations to help them understand the meaning of the new words.

- The students reread their own independent writing selections and look for opportunities to edit for word choice.

- Provide the students with a copy of familiar content area text. The students read and cross out words on their text, leaving only the important words. These key words are rewritten in a shortened form, much like a telegram, e-mail, or memorandum. The students tape record their shortened message for classmates.

### Additional Resources

Bear, D., Invernizzi, M., Templeton, S., & Johnston, F. *Words Their Way: Word Study for Phonics, Vocabulary, and Spelling Instruction.* Prentice Hall, 1999. ISBN 013021339X

Frasier, D. *Miss Alaineus: A Vocabulary Disaster.* Harcourt, 2000. ISBN 0152021639

Polacco, P. *Thundercake.* The Putnam & Gosset Publishing Group, 1997. ISBN 0698115813

Robb, L. *Easy Mini-Lessons for Building Vocabulary: Practical Strategies that Boost Word Knowledge and Reading Comprehension.* Scholastic, Inc., 1999. ISBN 0590264664

Swartz, S.L., & Yin, R. *Schools of Fish.* Dominie Press, Inc., 2001. ISBN 0768504813

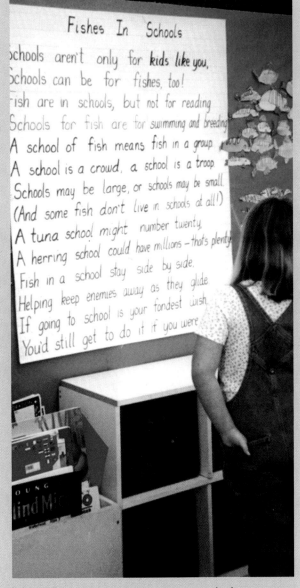

Rereading, concentrating on vocabulary.

# 12. Content Area

## Goal

The students will read familiar text in order to recognize and reinforce content area vocabulary.

## Basic Center

### Materials

Content area texts

Alphabet grid  (see Pages 158-159)

Pencil

### Preparation

The teacher will:

- Discuss how to identify the most important words that carry the meaning during shared reading and interactive writing.

- Demonstrate how to organize important words using an alphabet grid.

### Procedures

The students will:

- Reread familiar content area texts and select key vocabulary.

- Record important words or pictures alphabetically on individual grids.

Content area word bank.

- Read all the words/pictures and choose three. Discuss the meaning of each with a partner. The students use the word/picture in a sentence or act it out to convey understanding.

## Beyond the Basic Center

### Additional Center Ideas

- After repeated exposure to a story read aloud, record the text and place it in a listening center with puppets that represent the characters. The students listen to the tape. With a partner, they use puppets to retell the story, using vocabulary from the text.

- Prepare a variety of tongue depressors with a different cloze sentence (*He is a _____. Do you want a _____? Where is the _____?*) written on each depressor. Provide picture dictionaries and content area texts for reference. The students choose and read a cloze sentence. They decide on a word to complete the sentence and write the sentence in a content area journal. The students exchange journals and read each other's sentences.

- Set up a "Clipboard Cruising" center. Provide the students with individual clipboards and directions for a vocabulary search. The students "cruise" the room and read all available print (interactive writing, interactive editing, shared reading), searching for specific words or word parts as indicated on the provided direction card (content words, synonyms, base words, derivatives). The students record the words, exchange with a partner, and read for accuracy.

- Create a "Password" game, using content area vocabulary. After a unit of study, prepare strips of paper wide enough to fit inside an envelope. Write three content-specific words vertically on the strip. Seal an envelope with a window. Razor cut along the top and bottom of the envelope so the strip can be inserted and the words show through the window. The students play with a partner. Player 1 reads the first word on the strip to himself or herself and gives Player 2 a one-word clue in order to guess the word. The object is to guess the word with the least number of clues. The players alternate turns, inserting new vocabulary strips as necessary. Additional cards may be added when other topics are studied.

- The students individually reread a familiar content picture book. Using post-it notes, they mark several pages that contain content vocabulary that they wish to discuss with their friends. The reader gathers one or two classmates and reads the book aloud. The reader initiates discussion about the pre-marked vocabulary words.

### Additional Resources

Anderson, L. *Thank You, Sarah (The Woman Who Saved Thanksgiving)*. Simon & Schuster Books for Young Readers, 2002. ISBN 0689847874

Coles, R. *The Story of Ruby Bridges*. Scholastic, Inc., 1995. ISBN 0590572814

Erdrich, L. *Bears Make Rock Soup and Other Stories*. Children's Book Press, 2002. ISBN 0892391723

Gibbons, G. *The Reason for Seasons*. Holiday House, Inc., 1996. ISBN 0823412385

Hopkins, L. *Hand in Hand: An American History Through Poetry*. Simon & Schuster Children's, 1994. ISBN 067173315X

King, M. *I Have a Dream*. Scholastic, Inc., 1997. ISBN 0590205161

Mochizuki, K. *Passage to Freedom: The Sugihara Story*. Lee & Low Books, Inc., 1997. ISBN 1880000490

Tang, G. *The Best of Times (Math Strategies That Multiply)*. Scholastic, Inc., 2002. ISBN 0439210445

Wright-Frierson, V. *A Desert Scrapbook*. Aladdin Paperbacks, 2002. ISBN 0689850557

Yolen, J. *Encounter*. Harcourt, 1996. ISBN 015201389X

**Creating sentences.**

**Puppet center.**

**Clipboard cruising while concentrating on vocabulary.**

# 13. Math

## Goal
The students will read, represent, and communicate their understanding of simple mathematical stories.

## Basic Center

### Materials
Pocket Chart

Various mathematical story cards

Numerous picture cards

Numerous price tag cards

Several coin/dollar cards

### Preparation
The teacher will:

- Write a simple mathematical story on chart paper, such as: Tom bought three balls, two pencils, and one notebook at the store. The balls cost twenty-five cents each, the pencils cost ten cents each, and the notebook cost one dollar. How much money did Tom spend?

- Share read this story, think aloud, and model how to solve the problem.

**Organizing materials for a math center.**

- Demonstrate how to represent the math story, using pictures, price tags, and coin cards.

- Discuss the various problem solving strategies that could be used to solve this problem.

- Prepare other short math stories on individual task cards.

### Procedures
The students will:

- Work with a partner and take turns reading math stories.

- Organize picture cards, price tag cards, and coin/dollar cards to represent the written story.

- Determine the solution to the problem by observing their pictorial representation and discussing the story with their partner.

## Beyond the Basic Center

### Additional Center Ideas
- Make a pattern for a purse or wallet for the students to trace and cut out. Collect money stamps, stamp pads, and paper. Prepare task cards that show words and pictures of objects and their prices. Next they choose a task card with an object they would like to purchase and record the name and price on a slip of paper. Then they stamp the money needed to purchase the object and place the slip in their purse/wallet.

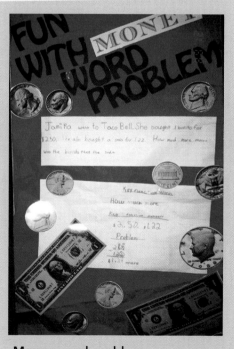

**Money word problems.**

- Prepare a clip art background on an overhead transparency and provide appropriate manipulatives. Collect a variety of math word problems (from textbooks, workbooks, or teacher resource books) that reflect the theme of the clip art background. Prepare individual word problem cards. The students work with a partner to select a card, read the problem, and represent the story, using manipulatives on the overhead.

- Prepare a math word bank using Velcro on a science display board. Collect a variety of photographs (math catalogs, workbooks, computer graphics) of math tools. Make small word labels to identify each math tool (blocks, calculator, scale). The students match the pictures to the correct label and attach them alphabetically to the word bank.

- Record a variety of word problems on sentence strips and collect pictures of math tools (scales, ruler, blocks). The students choose a sentence strip and place it in a pocket chart. Then they read the word problem and sort which tools could be used to solve the problem.

- Collect picture books and organize them in a basket. The students choose a book to read, using math vocabulary and concepts, and write an innovation.

## Additional Resources

Cato, S. *Addition.* Carolrhoda Books, Inc., 1999. ISBN 1575053209

Leedy, L. *The Monster Money Book.* Holiday House, Inc., 1992. ISBN 0823409228

Lewis, J. *Arithmetickle (An Even Number of Odd Riddle-Rhymes).* Harcourt, Inc., 2002. ISBN 0152164189

Schieszka, J., & Smith, L. *MATH CURSE.* Penguin Group, 1995. ISBN 0670861944

Tang, G. *Math for all Seasons (Mind-stretching Math Riddles).* Scholastic, Inc., 2002. ISBN 0439210429

Wells, R. *Bunny Money.* Dial Books for Young Readers, 1997. ISBN 0803721463

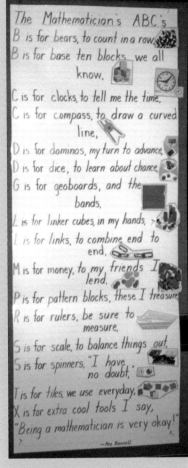

**The Mathematician's ABCs.**

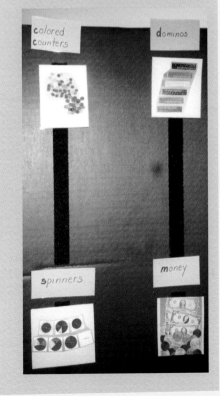

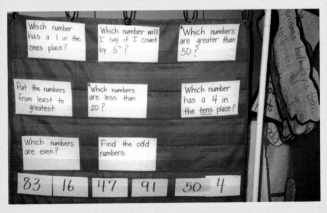

**A variety of math questions.**

# 14. Independent Reading

## Goal

The students will work together to practice and understand content area texts.

## Basic Center

### Materials

Multiple copies of familiar content area texts

### Preparation

The teacher will:

- Organize multiple copies of texts in containers for easy access.

- Model, during read aloud and shared reading, the processes (predicting, clarifying, summarizing, and questioning) readers use to comprehend a text.

- Teach the students how to share ideas, listen to one another, and respond to others' ideas about the book being discussed.

- Discuss with them how to divide the task of reading in a small group so that everyone participates.

### Procedures

The students will:

- Find people to read with and choose a text.

- Read the selected text together and verbally share ideas and questions.

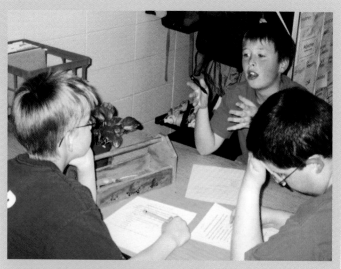

**Verbally sharing ideas.**

## Beyond the Basic Center

### Additional Center Ideas

- The students will choose a content area text to read together. After discussing important information, they will collaborate to create an artistic interpretation (mural, poster, or collage) representative of the text.

- After reading informational text together, the students will cooperatively discuss the text in order to summarize and write a brief news report. Plan time for them to share their newscast.

- Provide the students with large sheets of construction paper in order to write and design a book jacket. Book jackets should include both a written blurb that describes the text and an illustration.

- Start a KWL (Know, Want to know, Learn) chart during a unit of study and post it in the classroom. The students will read familiar content area texts relating to the unit of study and use post-it notes to add questions or information to the KWL chart.

- The students read texts together and clarify the information they've read. Working in pairs, they formulate multiple-choice questions with four possible answers. The test questions should be related to the main ideas in the text. The test questions may be posted so that other students can read and answer the questions.

### Additional Resources

Jones, C. *Mistakes That Worked*. Bantam Doubleday Dell Books for Young Readers, 1994. ISBN 0385320434

Leedy, L. *Postcards from Pluto*. Holiday House, Inc., 1997. ISBN 0823412377

Livingston, M., & Fisher, L. *Space Songs*. Holiday House, Inc., 1988. ISBN 082340675X

Schwartz, D. *G is for Googol*. Ten Speed Press, 1998. ISBN 1883672589

Schwartz, D. *Q is for Quark*. Ten Speed Press, 2001. ISBN 1582460213

Scieszka, J. *Math Curse*. Viking Children's Books, 1995. ISBN 0670861944

Reading content area texts together.

Swanson, D. *Animals Eat the Weirdest Things.* Henry Holt & Company, Inc., 1998. ISBN 080505846X

Westridge Young Writers Workshop. *Kids Explore Kids Who Make a Difference.* Avalon Travel Publishing, 1997. ISBN 1562613545

Wick, W. *A Drop of Water.* Scholastic, Inc., 1997. ISBN 0590221973

A unit of study KWL chart.

An artistic interpretation.

# 15. Nonfiction

## Goal
The students will reinforce strategies for reading informational text.

## Basic Center

### Materials
Familiar picture books

Multi-step direction chart

Construction paper

Markers, crayons, pencils

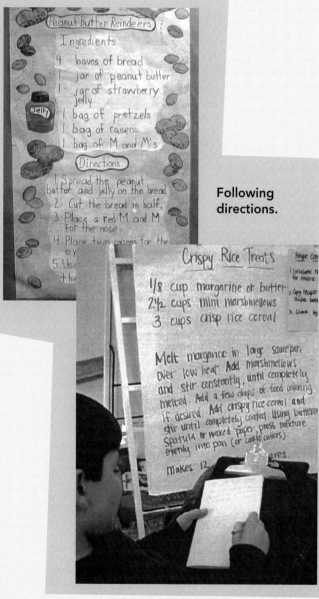

Following directions.

## Preparation
The teacher will:

- Share read simple directions. Discuss strategies for following written directions.

- Prepare a simple multi-step direction chart such as: Making a Book Jacket
  1. Find a book.
  2. Fold paper in half.
  3. Draw a picture about the book.
  4. Color the picture.

- Post the chart in the center.

## Procedures
The students will:

- Read the multi-step chart.

- Follow directions to complete the given task.

## Beyond the Basic Center

### Additional Center Ideas

- Prepare a shared reading that includes both a simple bar graph and incomplete statements about the graph. The students look at the graph and read the incomplete statements. Using the information provided on the graph, they complete the statements by inserting an appropriate word that describes the graph.

- Provide a recipe that relates to an idea or topic being studied. The students read and follow the recipe in order to assemble an edible treat.

- Collect a variety of menus and place them in a basket. The students select menus to read and order a meal. Then they role-play ordering the meal from a waiter or write down their own ideal menu choices.

- Collect a variety of reference materials (dictionaries, encyclopedias, brochures). The students locate and read additional information about the topic being studied in class. This information will provide the students with additional background to use in classroom discussions or projects.

- Gather school catalogs for the students to read. Using the index, they locate and list items that are necessary for classroom use.

## Additional Resources

Barnes, E. *Let's Have a Tea Party.* Harvest House Publishers, 1997. ISBN 1565076796

Better Homes and Gardens. *The New Junior Cookbook.* Better Homes and Gardens Books, 1997. ISBN 0696207087

Cianciolo, P. *Informational Picture Books for Children.* American Library Association, 1999. ISBN 0838907741

D'Amico, J., & Drummond, K. *The Math Chef.* John Wiley & Sons, Inc., 1997. ISBN 0471138134

Freeman, E., & Person, D. *Connecting Informational Children's Books with Content Area Learning.* Allyn & Bacon, Inc., 1997. ISBN 020526753X

Johnson, A. *The Buck Book (All Sorts of Things To Do With a Dollar Bill-Besides Spend It).* KLUTZ Publishing, 1993. ISBN 087192384X

Knapp, R. *Egyptian Art.* Davis Publications, Inc., 1998. ISBN 087192384X

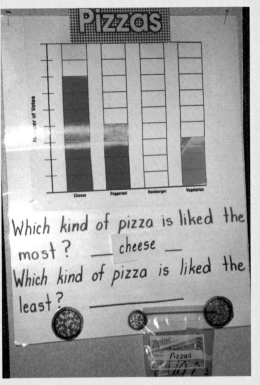

Create a bar graph to analyze.

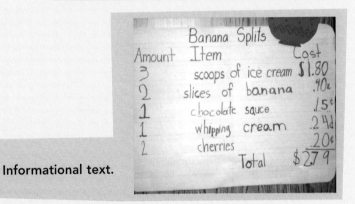

Informational text.

Role-play at a menu center.

# 16. Art

## Goal

The students will use artwork to illustrate concepts and interrelationships among concepts of a text they have read.

## Basic Center

### Materials

A piece of completed interactive writing

Paper (butcher, construction)

Paint

Paintbrushes

Clean-up materials

### Preparation

The teacher will:

- Plan, organize, and construct a piece of interactive writing related to a unit of study with the class.

- Post the finished interactive writing near the painting area.

### Procedures

The students will:

- Read the completed piece of interactive writing.

- Paint pictures that correspond to the interactive writing as decoration.

## Beyond the Basic Center

### Additional Center Ideas

- Provide a variety of art materials (watercolors, colored chalk, pastels, India ink, clay, markers, crayons) for the students to use in responding to a piece of literature or read aloud.

- Make/duplicate individual books that have text only. The students read the pages and illustrate them with stamps (rubber, sponge, student-made, potato). Upon completion, they reread the personalized books to a partner.

- With the students, share read a selection that has no pictures. Discuss what kinds of illustrations are needed to assist the reader. The students reread the text and create appropriate pictures, using a variety of

**Enhancing writing with art.**

art mediums. At a later time, attach the art to the shared reading selection.

- Through read aloud, shared reading, and interactive writing, study and discuss a famous artist. At the center, the students reread familiar material and create a rendition, using the artist's style. Provide necessary art materials that best represent the artist's medium.

- Provide the students with a familiar script. Working in small groups, they reread the script and determine the necessary props for a class presentation. Using a variety of art materials, they create appropriate headbands, puppets, scenery, costumes, and props.

### Additional Resources

Anholt, L. *Picasso and The Girl with a Ponytail: A Story About Pablo Picasso.* Barron's Educational Series, Inc., 1998. ISBN 0764150316

Arai, T. *Just Like Me.* Children's Book Press, 1997. ISBN 0892391499

DePaola, T. *The Art Lesson.* Putnam Publishing Group, 1997. ISBN 0698115724

Holub, J. *Vincent Van Gogh: Sunflowers and Swirly Stars.* Econo-Clad Books, 2001. ISBN 0613453204

Waldman, N. *Starry Night.* Boyd Mills Press, 1999.
ISBN 015201649X

Winter, J. *Diego.* Bantam Doubleday Dell Books for Young
Readers, 1994. ISBN 067985617X

Winter, J. *My Name is Georgia: A Portrait.* Harcourt, 1998.
ISBN 015201649X

Winter, J. *Frida.* Scholastic, Inc., 2002. ISBN 0590203207

**Making props for a class presentation.**

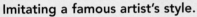

**Imitating a famous artist's style.**

**Responding to literature.**

**Stamp a story.**

# 17. Comprehension Strategies

## Goal
The students will use comprehension strategies as they read text.

## Basic Center

### Materials
Familiar read aloud text

Train cutouts

Paper

Pencil

### Preparation
The teacher will:

- Model the comprehension strategy of making connections orally, using the think aloud procedure.

- Involve the students in a discussion about how making personal connections enhances their understanding of a text.

- Prepare train cutouts for each student and write the title of a book on the train engine.

### Procedures
The students will:

- Reread a read aloud book and think about their personal connections to the text.

- Represent their personal connections by drawing a picture or writing their thoughts on the train cutout.

- Join their train car to those of their classmates, showing the many connections to the same text.

## Beyond the Basic Center

### Additional Center Ideas
- Collect a variety of texts (picture books, poetry, newspaper articles). Provide multiple copies of the form "Now I'm Thinking" (see Page 151). Organize the texts in a basket or tub. While the students read a text, they record their thought processes, changing ideas throughout the reading. They record their thoughts, using pictures, words, phrases, or sentences.

**A train full of connections.**

- The students work in pairs and reread a familiar text in order to practice the strategy of visualization. They take turns reading portions of texts aloud as their partner does a quick sketch of their visualization. Both the reader and the illustrator share their thinking before switching roles.

- The students practice monitoring and clarifying unfamiliar words, ideas, and phrases as they read aloud with a partner. They record clarifications and problem solving behaviors (rereading, background knowledge, glossary).

- The students use a sentence stem such as, "The important thing about _____ is _____" to record the main idea from a text. Sentences should be added to support their reasoning.

- As the students read assigned text, post-its are used to record their thinking. They write questions, connections, inferences, or any other important information used during their reading. After completing the reading, they join their group in order to compare and contrast their post-its. The students sort their individual post-its according to strategies used and compare them to others in the group.

## Additional Resources

Baylor, B. *I'm In Charge of Celebrations*. Econo-Clad Books, 1995. ISBN 0785783385

Brown, M. *The Important Book*. HarperCollins Publishers, 1990. ISBN 0064432270

Brown, M. *Another Important Book*. HarperCollins Publishers, 1999. ISBN 0060262826

Charlip, R. *Fortunately*. Simon & Schuster, 1993. ISBN 0689716605

Fox, M. *Wilfred Gorden McDonald Partridge*. Econo-Clad Books, 1989. ISBN 0613511072

Gray, L. *My Mama Had a Dancing Heart*. Scholastic, Inc., 1999. ISBN 0531071421

MacLachlan, P. *All The Places to Love*. HarperCollins Children's Books, 1994. ISBN 0060210982

Rylant, C. *When I Was Young in the Mountains*. Dutton Children's Books, 1985. ISBN 0140548750

**Good readers think about what they read.**

Student visualizations of text.

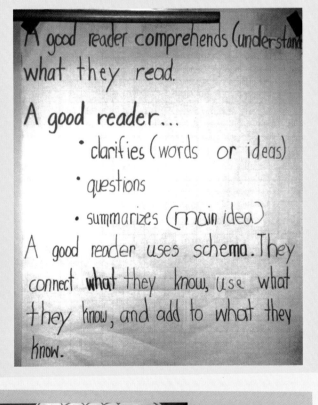

**Recording main ideas.**

Reading aloud with a partner.

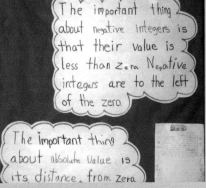

# 1. Making Books

## Goal

The students will use their knowledge of alphabetic principle to write their own books.

## Basic Center

### Materials

Classroom alphabet chart

Paper

Variety of writing and drawing materials

### Preparation

The teacher will:

- Read aloud a variety of alphabet books.

- Discuss the content and text structure used in an alphabet book.

- Determine with the class the pattern or structure to be followed in order to make a class alphabet book.

### Procedures

The students will:

- Choose a letter from the alphabet to write about, following the established pattern or structure.

- Illustrate a letter page for the class book.

## Beyond the Basic Center

### Additional Center Ideas

- Provide a variety of materials for the students to practice letter formation (glitter pens, paint, markers). As they complete a page of letters, assemble the pages and staple them into a book.

- Take a photograph of each student and duplicate it. Place the pictures in an envelope with the students' names printed on the front. Display the envelopes in a pocket chart. The students choose photos of their classmates in order to create a book of friends. They use alphabet stamps to stamp the first letter of their friend's name onto the top of a piece of paper. Then they glue the picture onto the middle of the page and write the friend's name at the bottom of the page. Finally, they arrange the pages alphabetically in individual books.

- Read several alphabet books and tongue twisters utilizing alliteration. Discuss the purpose and pattern

Making alphabet books.

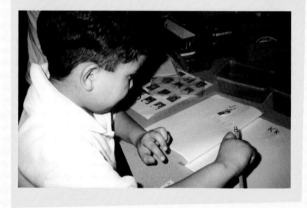

of alliteration. Prompt the students to write phrases using alliteration centered on a content area. (*Mature mathematicians manipulate materials to maximize their minds.*) The students choose a letter of the alphabet and an aspect of the content area and write their sentence. The pages are illustrated and compiled alphabetically into a class book.

- During a unit of study, create an alphabetical word bank. The students select one word from each letter of the alphabet bank. They write a sentence or sentences for each word selected. The sentence(s) should explain the significance of the word as it relates to the unit of study. Illustrate each page and assemble the pages to create an alphabet book.

- Using a word bank from a unit of study, the students write definitions for each word and organize them alphabetically in a class dictionary.

## Additional Resources

Bryan, A. *Ashley Bryan's ABC of African American Poetry*. Aladdin Paperbacks, 2001. ISBN 0689840454

Hiemen, S. *Egypt's ABCs: A Book about the People and Places of Egypt*. Picture Window Books, 2002. ISBN 1404800190

Hobbie, H. *Toot and Puddle: Puddle's ABC*. Little Brown & Company, 2000. ISBN 0316365939

Holabird, K. *Angelina Ballerina's ABC*. Pleasant Company Publications, 2002. ISBN 1584856130

McClintock, M. *Q Is for Duck: An Alphabet Guessing Game*. Houghton Mifflin Company, 1980. ISBN 0395300622

Merriam, E. *Spooky ABC*. Simon & Schuster Children's, 2002. ISBN 0689853564

Metropolitan Museum of Art. *Museum ABC*. Little, Brown & Company, 2002. ISBN 03160706

Shannon, G. *Tomorrow's Alphabet*. Econo-Clad Books, 1999. ISBN 0613181964

Tapahonso, L. *Navajo ABC: A Dine Alphabet Book*. Aladdin Paperbacks, 1999. ISBN 0689826850

Wilbur, R. *The Disappearing Alphabet*. Harcourt, Inc., 2001. ISBN 015216362X

Wood, A. *Alphabet Adventure*. Scholastic, Inc., 2001. ISBN 043908069X

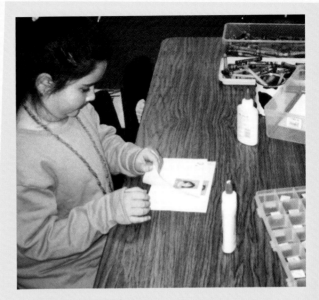

**A book of friends.**

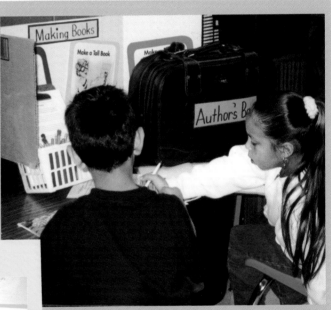

**Bookmaking center.**

**Class-made books.**

# 2. Skills Practice

## Goal

The students will practice a variety of skills to improve their writing, both in and out of context.

## Basic Center

### Materials

Various word cards (high frequency, high utility, content area)

White board

Dry erase markers

Eraser

### Preparation

The teacher will:

- Prepare word cards and organize materials.

- Demonstrate how to play the game "Mystery Word."
  **Game Directions:**
  1. The students form groups of three or four.
  2. Choose one student to be the writer.
  3. The writer chooses the "Mystery Word" from the stack of word cards.
  4. The writer writes only the first letter of the mystery word on the white board, using correct letter formation (manuscript or cursive).
  5. The players take turns guessing the mystery word.
  6. If a player guesses the mystery word correctly, the writer scribes the entire word on the white board. That player receives the word card and becomes the writer for the next "Mystery Word" game.
  7. If the players do not guess the mystery word, the writer writes the next letter of the mystery word. The same process continues until one player correctly guesses the mystery word.
  8. The object of the game is to collect the most word cards.

## Procedures

The students will:

- Find two or three students to play "Mystery Word."

- Play the game, paying close attention to letter formation when writing.

**Writing the Mystery Word.**

## Beyond the Basic Center

### Additional Center Ideas

- Provide the students with creative materials (chalk, shaving cream, pudding, sand) to practice correct letter formation.

- Gather plastic eggs and place them in an egg carton. Inside each egg place an upper case magnetic letter. The students open one egg at a time and identify the letter. They then record the upper case letter on a piece of paper, along with the corresponding lower case letter.

- Play the overhead game "Write On!" The students play with a partner to practice letter-sound correspondence. Using overhead letter tiles, Player 1 randomly chooses three tiles and puts them on the overhead. Next, the player turns on the overhead for five seconds as Player 2 writes the three letters on a piece of paper. Player 1 turns off the overhead, and Player 2 writes a word beginning with each letter. Player 1 turns the overhead back on and checks Player 2's words to be sure they start with each of the letters. If they are correct, the players say "Write On!" and alternate roles.

- Gather three blank dice or blocks. Write one word on each face of the dice/blocks. Use grade appropriate high frequency words. The students roll all three dice/blocks. Prepare a word graph record sheet for them to write the word each time it appears on the dice.

- Provide content area word bank, dictionary, digital timer, and dictionary record sheet (see Page 152). The students choose a word from the word bank, start the timer, and locate the word in the dictionary. Once the word has been located, they stop the timer and record the entry word, along with guide words from the dictionary and the amount of time taken to complete the task. The goal is for them to be able to quickly locate words in a dictionary.

Matching eggs.

### Additional Resources

Clements, A. *The School Story*. Simon & Schuster Books for Young Readers, 2001. ISBN 0689825943

Dakos, K. *Don't Read This Book Whatever You Do!* Aladdin Paperbacks, 1993. ISBN 0689821328

Harwayne, S. *Messages to Ground Zero*. Heinemann Publishers, 2002. ISBN 0325005141

Howe, D. *Bunnicula: A Rabbit-Tale of Mystery*. Simon & Schuster Children's, 1996. ISBN 0689806590

Prellar, J. *The Case of the Million-Dollar Mystery*. Scholastic, Inc., 2002. ISBN 0439426294

Rylant, C. *Every Living Thing*. Aladdin Paperbacks, 1985. ISBN 0689712634

Travis, F. *Great Book of Whodunit Puzzles: Mini-Mysteries for You to Solve*. Sterling Publishing Company, Inc., 1993. ISBN 0806903481

Van Allsberg, C. *The Mysteries of Harris Burdick*. Houghton Mifflin Company, 1984. ISBN 0395353939

High frequency word roll.

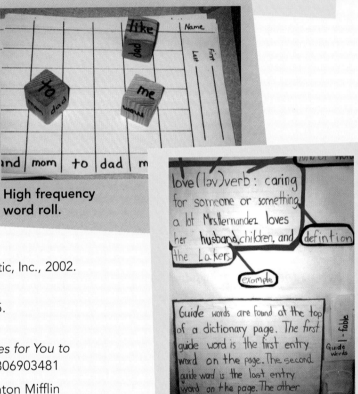
Practicing dictionary skills.

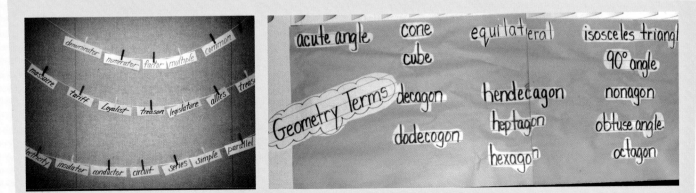
Content area word walls for writing reference.

# 3. Newspapers

## Goal

The students will use knowledge of concepts of print to write informational text.

## Basic Center

### Materials

Examples of newspapers

Newsprint paper

Variety of writing tools

Computer with suitable software for creating a newspaper (optional)

### Preparation

The teacher will:

- Post an example of a newspaper selection that was created during interactive writing or introduced during shared reading close to the center.

- Create a newspaper template on an 8½" x 11" piece of paper that corresponds to the format studied.

- Gather materials necessary for the center and organize them into accessible containers.

### Procedures

The students will:

- Contribute selections to a class newspaper, using the created template, computer program, or newsprint paper.

- Edit their writing for informational text format and conventions (column text, headlines, subheadings, boldfaced print, picture placement, captions).

## Beyond the Basic Center

### Additional Center Ideas

- Reproduce comic strips from a newspaper and cover the text. The students write new text for the comic strips.

- The students determine and write questions for a survey. At a specified time, they conduct the survey and record the information. Then they tally the information and decide how to report the findings by using a picture, chart, or graph. A written summary will accompany the data.

- Establish an advice column where the students contribute letters expressing class or school concerns. Provide a box where they can leave their letters. Other students choose letters to answer that will later be published in the class newspaper.

- The students use persuasive writing style to create reviews of food, movies, books, or school policies.

- The students conduct interviews using predetermined questions or those they have written themselves. They may interview school personnel, relatives, friends, or community members. The students compile interview information into a biographical news article.

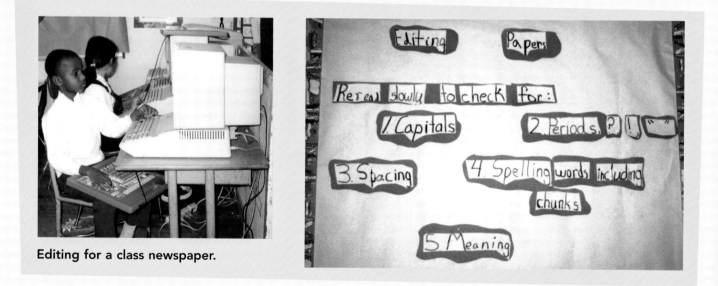

Editing for a class newspaper.

## Additional Resources

Crosby, D. *Create your Own Class Newspaper: A Complete Guide for Planning, Writing & Publishing a Newspaper.* Incentive Publications Inc., 1999. ISBN 0865302898

Gibbons, G. *Deadline! From News to Newspaper.* HarperCollins Children's Books, 1987. ISBN 0690046022

Leedy, L. *The Furry News: How to Make a Newspaper.* Holiday House, Inc., 1996. ISBN 0823410269

McGuder, A. *The Boondocks: Because I Know You Don't Read the Newspapers.* Andrews McMeel Publishing, 2000. ISBN 0740706098

Pilkey, D. *Dog Breath! The Horrible Terrible Trouble with Hally Tosis.* Blue Sky Press, 1994. ISBN 0590474669

Pilkey, D. *The Paperboy.* Scholastic, Inc., 1999. ISBN 0531071391

Rylant, C. *Some Good News.* Simon & Schuster Children's, 2001. ISBN 0689817126

**Planning for the class newspaper.**

**Locating a comic strip to rewrite.**

**Conducting surveys.**

# 4. Graphic Organizers

## Goal

The students will practice the process of organizing information to facilitate independent writing.

## Basic Center

### Materials

Web organizer (see Page 153)

Writing materials

Sentence frames

Information to organize (pictures, words, sentences, paragraphs)

### Preparation

The teacher will:

- Interactively create a web based on a curricular topic.

- Determine and display a sentence frame for the web. (A duck has _____. Exploration was influenced by _____.)

- Model how to generate and sort information from a topic, using the pictures, words, and/or sentences gathered throughout the unit.

- Store collected pictures, words, and/or sentences from the unit of study in a container.

### Procedures

The students will:

- Use the information provided to complete the web organizer.

- Use the sentence frame to create additional sentences about the web.

## Beyond the Basic Center

### Additional Center Ideas

- Use interactive writing to create a Venn diagram along with a summary statement. The students use yarn to create their own Venn diagrams. They then organize pictures, words, or sentences that relate to the current unit of study.

Preparing content area webs.

- Conduct surveys with the students. Organize the information with various types of graphic organizers (bar graphs, pie graphs, pictographs). Use interactive writing to summarize the information. The students then graph the data from other surveys, using the graphic organizers, and write a summary statement for each one.

- Use a tablecloth and colored tape to create a grid for a chart. The students sort information based on the current unit of study or literature classifications (pictures of animals—farm vs. jungle; titles of books by text type or theme; texts—features of nonfiction, elements of a narrative).

- Conduct an interactive editing lesson. Record the key words on note cards. The students then sort the cards and organize the information into sentences or paragraphs.

- To help the students recognize text organization, take a familiar shared reading text and use interactive editing to identify key concepts. Record the key concepts in the form of an outline. The students then use this same procedure to create outlines, using other familiar texts at the center.

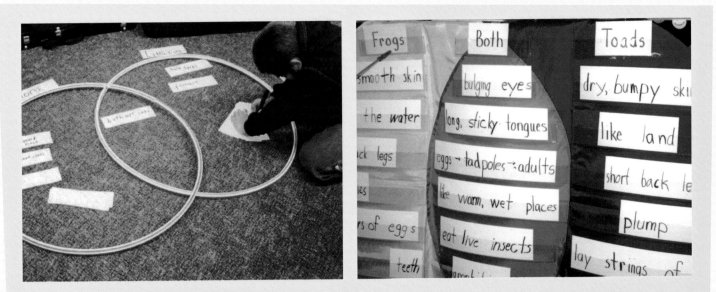

An interactive editing lesson identifying key words.

## Additional Resources

Drapeau, P. *Great Teaching with Graphic Organizers: Lessons & Fun-Shaped Templates that Motivate Kids of All Learning Styles.* Scholastic, Inc., 1999. ISBN 0590128760

Murphy, S. *The Best Vacation Ever.* HarperCollins Children's Books, 1997. ISBN 064467066

Murphy, S. *Lemonade For Sale.* HarperCollins Publishers, 1997. ISBN 0064467155

Creating a Venn diagram.

# 5. Text Features

## Goal

The students will recognize text features and utilize them when writing.

## Basic Center

### Materials

Numerous pictures (magazines, newspapers, photocopies)

3 pieces of 8½" x 11" paper folded and stapled as a book

A variety of writing tools

Collection of nonfiction texts

### Preparation

The teacher will:

- Read aloud a variety of nonfiction texts, discussing captions as a feature of text.

- Use a previous interactive writing and add pictures with captions.

- Collect pictures around a nonfiction theme and organize them.

### Procedures

The students will:

- Choose six pictures and glue one picture on each page of the prepared book.

- Write a caption (word, phrase, sentence) for each picture.

- Write a title and a title page for the book.

- Read the book to a partner.

## Beyond the Basic Center

### Additional Center Ideas

- The students independently read books of their choice. Prepare an author/illustrator recording log. The students record books read by title, author, and illustrator.

- Prepare an overhead transparency of the table of contents from a nonfiction book. Collect multiple copies of the book and provide clipboards for the students. The students work in small groups at the overhead. One student acts as the teacher and uses

Creating captions for pictures.

the table of contents, asking the other students to look for specific information. The students locate the information in the books and record page numbers. The students check each other for accuracy.

- Provide a variety of diagrams depicting quantitative information related to the current unit of study (average rainfall, census figures, Revolutionary War casualties). Use this information to create a chart.

- Provide a variety of nonfiction texts relating to a unit of study. With a partner, or in small groups, identify key words. Organize the words into a glossary, defining each word.

- As a culminating activity for a unit of study, work in pairs to co-author a book highlighting information learned. In addition to the narrative text, the book must include the following features: title page, table of contents, pictures with captions, graphs, and a glossary.

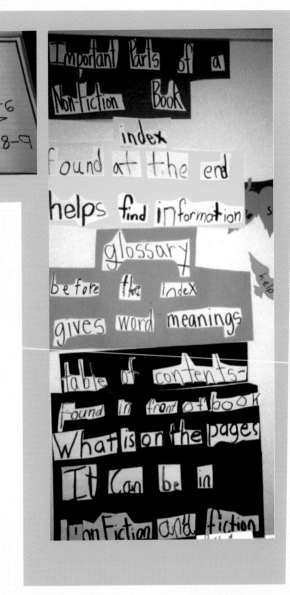

Text features.

## Additional Resources

Barnes, K. *How It Works: The Human Body.* Barnes & Noble Books, 1997. ISBN 0760704287

Canfield, J. *Chicken Soup for the Preteen Soul: 101 Stories of Changes, Choices and Growing Up for Kids Ages 9-13.* Health Communications, Inc., 2000. ISBN 1558748008

Cooper, C. *MATTER: Eyewitness Books.* DK Publishing, Inc., 1992. ISBN 0789448866

Egan, V. *101 Questions and Answers: World of Knowledge.* Barnes & Noble Books, 1997. ISBN 0760704104

Osbourne, W. *Titantic: A Nonfiction Guide to Tonight on the Titanic.* Random House Children's Books, 2002. ISBN 0375813578

Petty, K. *The Super Science Book.* Random House, 2002. ISBN 1357918642

Randall, R. *The Children's Book of Myths and Legends: Extraordinary Stories from Around the World.* Barnes & Noble Books, 2001. ISBN 076072542X

Co-authoring a book at the writing center.

# 6. Names

## Goal

The students will use their knowledge of letters and sounds from their own names and the names of their friends and apply that knowledge when writing new words.

## Basic Center

### Materials

Sentence strips with the students' names and photos

Task cards with a variety of phonic patterns associated with names

Paper

Variety of writing tools

Clipboards

### Preparation

The teacher will:

- Organize materials by putting name strips into a plastic bag, envelope, or box.

- Model how the names the students know help them to write new words during interactive writing.

Sequencing letters in your name.

- Prepare task cards that focus on phonic patterns that have been studied. (Find words that have the letter *S*, as in *Stephanie*. Find words that have a long e sound, as in *Mary*, *Steve*, *Chelsea*, and *Katie*).

### Procedures

The students will:

- Choose a task card. The students record the names used and highlight the phonic pattern on paper.

- Search the room for the designated phonic pattern and record words that correspond with the pattern found in the name.

## Beyond the Basic Center

### Additional Center Ideas

- Provide a variety of art media, (alphabet macaroni, clay, chalk, paint, markers, stickers, alphabet stamps) for the students to use in recording their own and their friends' names.

- Prepare individual name cards for each student. The students sort the names by the number of syllables and record these on a sheet (see Page 147). They later sort the words from the word wall in the same way and record them.

- Create individual dictionaries to help the students make letter-sound connections to the names of their classmates. Prepare a book with one page for each letter of the alphabet and photocopy individual

### Identifying names with phonic patterns

photos of the students. The students sort their classmates' photos and place them on the appropriate page. They may write their classmate's name or the beginning letter beneath the picture. The students may later sort other pictures from magazines and add them to the appropriate pages or add written words.

- The students create acrostic poems, using their own names or names of classmates, book characters, or historical figures. Encourage them to write poems at the word, phrase, or sentence level.

- Create name word banks by utilizing important names from the current content study (presidents, inventors, book characters). Use these as additional resources for word analysis.

## Additional Resources

Bayer, J. *A My Name is Alice.* Penguin Putnam Books for Young Readers, 1987. ISBN 0140546685

Catalanotto, P. *Matthew ABC.* Simon & Schuster Children's, 2002. ISBN 0689845820

Choi, Y. *The Name Jar.* Random House Books for Young Readers, 2001. ISBN 037580613X

Henkes, K. *Chrysanthemum.* William Morrow & Co., 1996. ISBN 0688147321

Levine, E. *If Your Name Was Changed At Ellis Island.* Scholastic, Inc., 1994. ISBN 0590438298

Rylant, C. *The Old Woman Who Named Things.* Harcourt, 2000. ISBN 0152021027

Recording friends' names.

Using famous names.

Acrostic poem.

Names by syllables.

# 7. Word Work

## Goal

The students will practice using the relationship between letters and sounds to reinforce known words and to create new words.

## Basic Center

### Materials

Timer

High frequency words displayed on a word wall

Clipboard

Paper

### Preparation

The teacher will:

- Build a word wall of high frequency words in the classroom.

- During interactive writing and shared reading, choose high frequency words to gradually add to the wall.

- Directly instruct the students in strategies for learning new words.

### Procedures

The students will:

- Position themselves with a clipboard, paper, pencil, and timer near the word wall.

- Write as many words as possible from the word wall in a specified amount of time.

- Have a friend check the words for accuracy.

## Beyond the Basic Center

### Additional Center Ideas

- Prepare individual envelopes with the students' names (content area words, famous names, spelling words) on the front. Put individual letters for each word inside the envelope. The students choose envelopes, sequence the letters, and record the words.

- Organize magnetic letters in a divided plastic box. Provide a collection of words that contain the most frequent rimes. The students choose a card and spell the word, using the magnetic letters. Next they

**Writing known words.**

record the word on a sheet of paper. Then the students manipulate the magnetic letters by removing the onset and replacing it with other letter combinations to make and record new words (*cat/mat/bat/flat/scat*).

- Create individual spelling books. As the students learn about different spelling patterns, a resource page is created to record examples of different ways to spell similar sounds (rela*tion*, comprehen*sion*, *ocean*, suspi*cion*).

- Using the student name chart, highlight and discuss specific spelling patterns (*Charity, Cheryl, Christopher*). The students then locate examples of the spelling pattern in other words, using the print in the classroom. The students categorize the words by sound and record the ones they find.

- Create and post content area word banks during interactive writing and interactive editing. On different days, model sorting words according to a variety of phonic patterns. The students use familiar word banks to sort and record words by a phonic pattern. They give their recorded list to a friend, who must write the phonic rule (*addition, addend, add, answer*, all have a short *a* sound).

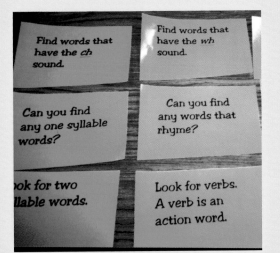

Examples of task cards.

Using task cards.

## Additional Resources

Dobkin, B. *Go With Words.* Scholastic Library Publishing, 2000. ISBN 0516220314

Hajdusiewicz, B. *Words and More Words: A Reference for Young Writers.* Addison-Wesley, 1997. ISBN 06733633201

Rodgers, R. *My Favorite Things.* HarperCollins Children's Books, 2001. ISBN 0060287101

Taback, S. *This is the House That Jack Built.* Penguin USA, 2002. ISBN 0399234888

Wells, R. *Letters and Sounds.* Penguin Putnam Books for Young Readers, 2001. ISBN 0140568050

Wilbur, R. *Pig in the Spigot.* Harcourt, 2000. ISBN 0152020195

Sorting words.

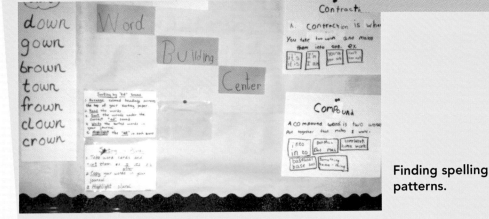

Finding spelling patterns.

# 8. Vocabulary

## Goal
The students will participate in word study activities in order to learn and use new vocabulary in their writing.

## Basic Center

### Materials
White board

Dry erase markers

Eraser

Picture and/or word cards related to content

Giving clues in order to "Picture This."

### Preparation
The teacher will:

- Prepare picture/word cards organized by categories (clothing, furniture, states). These words may come from content area word banks.

- Plan read alouds and interactive writing lessons to familiarize the students with riddles. Use words from word banks to write riddles.

- Demonstrate how to play the game "Picture This" by describing an object from the word bank, using its attributes.

    **Game Directions:**
    1. The students play in pairs.
    2. Player 1 chooses a picture/word card and thinks of attributes to describe the object. Player 1 says, "Picture This" and orally gives one clue about the word/picture.

3. Player 2 uses a white board and marker to record a guess of the answer to the "Picture This" riddle.
4. Player 2 shows the board to Player 1 and reads the guess aloud. If the guess is correct, the two players switch roles. If the guess is incorrect, Player 1 gives additional clues one at a time until Player 2 correctly identifies the word/picture.

## Procedures
The students will:

- Find a partner and choose a group of cards.

- Play "Picture This," trying to use precise language and giving as few clues as possible for a partner to guess the riddle.

Writing riddles using interesting vocabulary.

## Beyond the Basic Center

### Additional Center Ideas

- Prepare a restaurant center with menus, props, and order pads. The students assume the roles of the customer and server. Customers read and order from the menu while the server writes the order.

- Gather an assortment of magazines. The students search for pictures that correspond to a given category (tools, ocean animals, school supplies). On a large sheet of paper, they write the category and glue chosen pictures. The students write labels or captions for pictures to create a personal word bank.

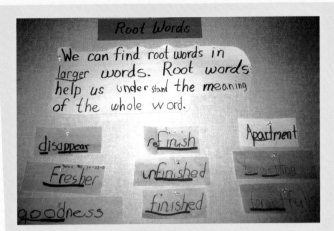

Study the root words for meaning.

- Use interactive editing to begin a content area word bank. Post the word bank where the students can easily access it as a resource. Provide graph paper for the students to create a word search, using the content area words. The students solve each other's word searches.

- Read aloud and discuss books that contain idiomatic expressions. Demonstrate how to use an idiom dictionary to find meanings of unusual expressions. Prepare sentence strips with a variety of idiomatic expressions. The students choose an idiom to write in a sentence and illustrate. Provide an idiom dictionary as a resource. Illustrations may be serious or comical.

- Encourage the students to look for words that have common derivatives. Discuss word origins and the fact that many English words have Greek or Latin roots. Explore this principle, using interactive writing. Prepare word cards that contain common roots (*bio, geo, graph*) and star-shaped pieces of paper. The students choose a word card and write the root in the center of the star, along with its meaning. On the other points of the star, the students generate other words that have the same root. Provide a dictionary as a resource.

### Additional Resources

Brown, M. *The Important Book.* HarperCollins Publishers, 1951. ISBN 0060207205

Charlip, R. *Fortunately.* Simon & Schuster, 1993. ISBN 0689716605

Frasier, D. *Miss Alaineus: A Vocabulary Disaster.* Harcourt, 2000. ISBN 0152021639

Fry, E., Kress, J., & Fountoukidis, D. *The Reading Teacher's Book of Lists,* Third Edition. Prentice-Hall, Inc., 1993. ISBN 0130348937

Hambleton, V. *So, You Wanna Be a Writer?: How to Write, Get Published, and Maybe Even Make It Big!* Beyond Words Publishing, 2001. ISBN 1582700435

Lassen, C. R. *Sea Treasures.* The Book Company, 2001. ISBN 1740470664

Terban, M. *Dictionary of Idioms (More Than 600 Phrases, Sayings, and Expressions).* Scholastic, 1996. ISBN 0590381571

Young, S. *The Scholastic RHYMING Dictionary.* Scholastic, Inc., 1994. ISBN 0590494600

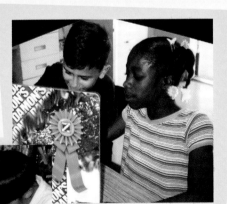

Create a restaurant center.

# 9. Spelling

## Goal
The students will practice and apply their knowledge of phonics as they spell words in their writing.

## Basic Center

### Materials
Word wall (high frequency and high utility words)

Gel pens in a variety of colors

Independent writing selections

### Preparation
The teacher will:

- Use a familiar shared reading text or a completed interactive writing text to locate word wall words.

- Demonstrate how to locate words found in the text and the word wall.

- Model how to recognize and rewrite the word wall words, tracing over the same word repeatedly with the gel pens and using three different colors to "Rainbow Write."

### Procedures
The students will:

- Use a piece of their own independent writing to recognize and locate word wall words.

- Check the spelling of the word.

- "Rainbow Write" by tracing over the word three times, using a different color pen each time.

## Beyond the Basic Center

### Additional Center Ideas
- Practice spelling high frequency words, using a variety of media (glitter, beans, yarn).

- The students make an onset and rime flip book. Provide sentence strips, markers, and a stapler. The students choose a high utility word (*day, still, can*) from the word wall and write it on a sentence strip. Then they write onsets on sentence strips, cutting the strips after each onset. They staple all the onsets on top of the original word to make the flipbook. The students leave the book for others to read.

- Play "Word Detective" in pairs. Player 1 chooses a word wall word and formulates three clues about

**Locating word wall words.**

that word. Player 1 tells Player 2 the first clue. ("My word has two vowels.") Player 2 writes all the words from the word wall that apply to this clue. Player 1 reveals the second clue. ("There is a consonant between the two vowels.") Player 2 circles the words on the list that still apply. Player 1 gives the last clue. ("The final vowel is silent.") Player 2 underlines the words that continue to apply and makes a guess. The players take turns acting as the "Word Detective."

- Using word wall words and/or spelling words, sort the words according to specifically assigned criteria (blends, digraphs, syllables, prefixes, suffixes). Complete the record sheet labeled "All Sorts of Words" (see Page 154) and represent the sort on the graph.

- Using content area words, the students sort by prefixes and suffixes (*un-, non-, -ful, -ment*). On a graphic organizer, the students sort and rewrite words that have similar meanings.

### Additional Resources
Abdelnoor, J. *The Silver Burdett Mathematical Dictionary.* Silver Burdett Press, 1979. ISBN 0382093097

*American Heritage Student Science Dictionary.* Houghton Mifflin, 2002. ISBN 061818919X

Bridwell, N. *Clifford the Big Red Dog: Magnet Spelling.* Scholastic, Inc., 2002. ISBN 0439332435

Rime flip books.

Practicing word wall words with yarn.

Cunningham, P., & Allington, R. *Classrooms That Work: They Can All Read and Write* (3rd Edition). Pearson Education, 2002. ISBN 0205355412

Cunningham, P. *Phonics They Use: Words for Reading and Writing* (3rd Edition). Addison-Wesley, 1999. ISBN 0321020553

Nilsen, A. *I Can Spell Words With Three Letters.* Houghton Mifflin, 1998. ISBN 0753451247

Terban, M. *The Scholastic Dictionary of Spelling.* Scholastic, Inc., 2000. ISBN 0439144965

Wittels, H. *How to Spell It: A Handbook of Commonly Misspelled Words.* Putnam Publishing Group, 1981. ISBN 0448147564

Making words using prefixes and suffixes.

# 10. Letter Writing

## Goal
The students will practice standard conventions and formats used in writing letters for a variety of purposes.

## Basic Center

### Materials
Paper in different sizes, shapes, and colors

Variety of writing utensils

Envelopes

### Preparation
The teacher will:

• Post an example of a letter that was created during interactive writing or introduced during shared reading close to the center.

• Organize materials in letter trays, pencil holders, file folders, baskets, or any other suitable containers.

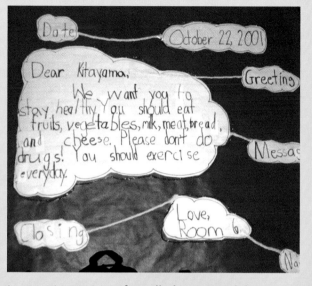

**Interactive writing friendly letter model.**

### Procedures
The students will:

• Write letters, using the posted model as a resource.

• Edit their writing for proper format (friendly letter, business letter, thank-you note, memo) and written language conventions.

## Beyond the Basic Center

### Additional Center Ideas
• Involve the students in designing and decorating a large cardboard box to resemble a post office. Have them take turns being the postmaster, selling stamps, processing letters, and delivering mail.

• Use interactive writing to contact others and establish pen pals. Potential pen pals include anyone who might respond and continue a correspondence. Provide materials and a time line for the students to write to their pen pals.

• Based on content area study, have the students write letters to storybook characters or influential historical figures. They may ask questions regarding the recipients' feelings or actions and events that occurred in the text. They may also respond by sharing their personal connections or reactions.

• Create a Card Design Center. Collect various kinds of greeting cards, thank-you notes, and invitations and make them available for the students to use as format examples. Include art supplies for them to illustrate and decorate their cards.

• As the students become proficient with basic letter formats, have them write letters for different purposes. They can write letters to invite their parents to school events, inform their family members of what they have learned in school, or make requests. Older students can write persuasive letters to local newspapers or politicians.

### Additional Resources
Ada, A. *Dear Peter Rabbit*. Simon & Schuster Children's, 1994. ISBN 0689318502

Ada, A. *Yours Truly, Goldilocks*. Simon & Schuster Children's, 1998. ISBN 0689816081

Ada, A. *With Love, Little Red Hen*. Simon & Schuster Children's, 2001. ISBN 0689825811

Hesse, K., Rosen, M., et al. *When I Was Your Age (Stories About Growing Up, Vol. 2)*. Candlewick Press, 1999. ISBN 0763604070

Klise, K. *Regarding the Fountain: A Tale, in Letters, of Liars and Leaks.* HarperCollins Publishers, 1999. ISBN 0380793474

Leedy, L. *Messages in the Mailbox: How to Write a Letter.* Holiday House, Inc., 1994. ISBN 082341079X

O'Conner, J. *Dear Tooth Fairy*, Vol. 2. Penguin Putnam Books for Young Readers, 2002. ISBN 0448428490

Schimmel, S. *Dear Children of the Earth: A Letter from Home.* Creative Publishing International, 1994. ISBN 0765569779

Stanley, D. *Raising Sweetness.* Penguin Putnam Books, 2002. ISBN 0698119622

**Role-playing in the post office.**

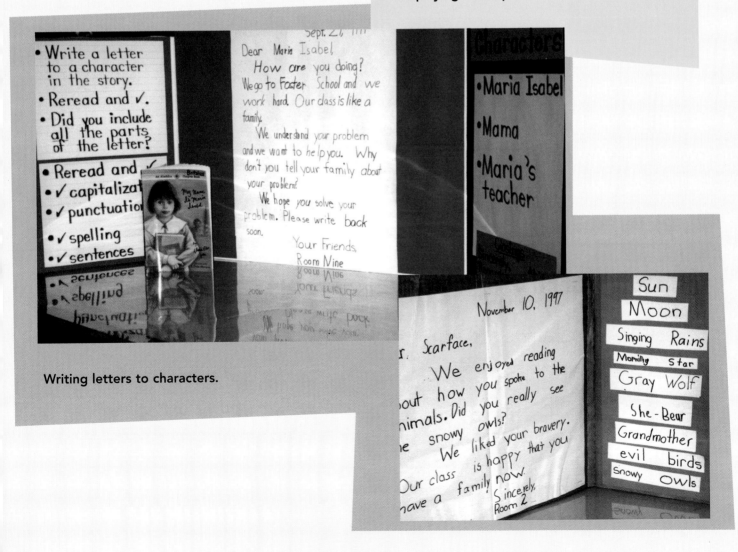

**Writing letters to characters.**

# 11. Technology

## Goal
The students will use a variety of technologies to produce and enhance written text.

## Basic Center

### Materials
Computer

Word processing program

Printer

A single piece of familiar text (rhyme or poem)

Decorative computer paper

### Preparation
The teacher will:

- Work with the selected text over several days during shared reading, interactive writing, and/or interactive editing.

- Place the familiar text next to a computer.

- Teach the students basic computer operations.

- Provide the students with strategies for accurate copying of text.

### Procedures
The students will:

- Read the text.

- Accurately type the selected text.

- Reread the text, paying attention to written language conventions (capitalization, punctuation, spacing).

- Select appropriate clip art to represent the meaning of the text.

- Print the text on decorative computer stationery.

- Read the text to a partner.

## Beyond the Basic Center

### Additional Center Ideas
- The students make gifts to present to someone special in their lives. They choose an appropriate text that has a meaningful connection to their special person. They write a personal dedication, explaining the reason the text was selected for the

**Working together on the computer.**

recipient. Then they edit and type the dedication and text, add appropriate clip art, and choose decorative computer stationery and a frame.

- The students independently write a story that will be published for the class library. After editing, they type their stories on the computer. The published book should include appropriate book conventions (table of contents, dedication, glossary).

- Taking a familiar shared reading, interactive writing, or interactive editing text, the students create an innovation by substituting selected words from the text with their own words. They type their innovations and edit them, using spellcheck.

- For an oral presentation, the students select a familiar poem to recite for an audience. They type and edit their selection and print it on an overhead transparency. Based on the students' interpretations of the poem, they select music to accompany the presentation.

- The students select a current article from a newspaper or magazine. They use interactive editing to identify key points from the article. Then they use these key points and add graphics to design a PowerPoint transparency. A computer and LCD projector may also be used, if they are available.

## Additional Resources

Fleischman, P. *BIG TALK*. Candlewick Press, 2000. ISBN 0763606367

Goldish, M. *Thematic Poems Songs and Fingerplays*. Scholastic, Inc., 1993. ISBN 0590496387

Katz, B. *We the People*. Greenwillow, 2000. ISBN 068816532X

Moore, H. *A Poem a Day*. Scholastic, Inc., 1997. ISBN 0590294334

Myers, T. *Basho and the Fox*. Cavendish Publishers, 2000. ISBN 0761450688

Prelutsky, J. *It's Raining Pigs & Noodles*. Greenwillow, 2000. ISBN 006029195

Silverstein, S. *Where the Sidewalk Ends (25th Anniversary Edition)*. HarperCollins, 2000. ISBN 0060291699

Yolen, J. *Color Me a Rhyme*. Boyd Mills Press, 2000. ISBN 056397892X

Reciting a poem for an audience.

Preparing a PowerPoint presentation.

Getting ready to publish written work.

# 12. Research

## Goal

The students will review and learn new information. They will write to communicate what they've learned, demonstrating knowledge of written language conventions.

## Basic Center

### Materials

Content area texts at varying levels of difficulty

Paper

Writing tools

Art materials

### Preparation

The teacher will:

- Share read and discuss a variety of nonfiction texts.
- Determine and highlight key vocabulary.
- Work with the students to write paraphrases that include key vocabulary.
- Discuss this strategy with the students as a way to record written information without plagiarizing other people's work.

### Procedures

The students will:

- Read text(s) in the same subject area to learn new information on a topic of interest.

- Identify key vocabulary and write paraphrases.
- Construct grade appropriate text.
- Proofread, edit, and publish their text.

## Beyond the Basic Center

### Additional Center Ideas

- The students read content area print available in the room and search for high frequency words. First they use Wikki Stix, to highlight words. Next, they proofread their own writing, using Wikki Stix to highlight appropriate use of high frequency words, and have a friend check for accuracy.

- The students write sentences related to the content area being studied and use a sentence pattern. ( _____ are rectangles.) They use capital letters at the beginning of the sentence and ending punctuation appropriately. Then they illustrate each sentence.

- Interactively write a class editing rubric and display it in the classroom as a resource. Provide student content area writing from other classrooms (with no names). In pairs, the students read and edit the writing, using the rubric as a guide. Then they rewrite and copy the text and leave it in a folder at the center for other students to review. Additional students at the center will examine and continue to edit the text. The text will then be used for a whole group discussion on how written language conventions and editing impact their writing.

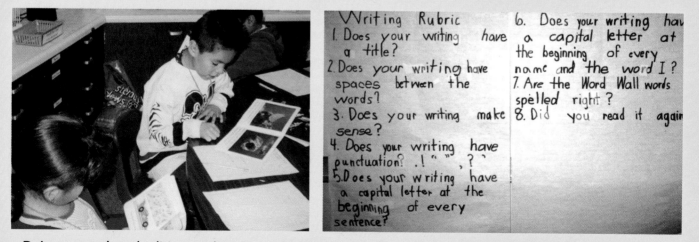

Doing research and editing work.

- The students identify key words from a content text. Then they sort the key words into categories by meaning. They record the categories and words on a graphic organizer. The students then use the organizer to write a research paper, using the categorized words.

- Write content-based sentences on sentence strips. Display the strips randomly in a pocket chart. In pairs, the students organize the sentence strips into a coherent text structure (bulleted list, paragraph, letter). They negotiate and write a beginning sentence for the text. They transcribe the text, using a word processor, and add the text to their other writing and research involved in the unit of study.

**Using Wikki Stix to locate known words.**

**Conducting an investigation for research.**

## Additional Resources

Barchers, S. *Cooking Up U.S. History: Recipes and Research to Share with Children.* Teacher Ideas Press, 1999. ISBN 1563086824

Borne, B. *100 Research Topic Guides for Students.* Greenwood Publishing Group, Inc., 1996. ISBN 0313295522

Meyer, V. *Write Source 2000: A Guide to Writing, Thinking and Learning.* Great Source Education Group, 1999. ISBN 066946774X

Montgomery, S. *The Snake Scientist.* Houghton Mifflin Company, 2001. ISBN 0618111190

Osbourne, W. *Space: A Nonfiction Companion to Midnight on the Moon.* Bantam Doubleday Dell Books for Young Readers, 2002. ISBN 037581356X

Schrecengost, M. *Researching Events.* Highsmith Press, LLC, 1998. ISBN 1579500188

Swartz, S.L., Shook, R.E., & Klein, A.F. *Interactive Writing and Interactive Editing.* Dominie Press, Inc., 2001. ISBN 0768505348

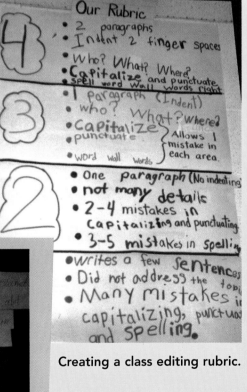

**Creating a class editing rubric.**

**Organizing sentence strips.**

# 13. Response to Literature

## Goal
The students will read various literature selections and demonstrate comprehension by responding in a written form.

## Basic Center

### Materials
Books used during guided reading, book clubs, or independent reading

Paper (literature response logs, optional)

Pencils, crayons, or markers

### Preparation
The teacher will:

- Model the use of comprehension strategies, using a think aloud strategy as the texts are read in class.

- Encourage the students to use comprehension strategies as they participate in conversations during read aloud, guided reading, and book clubs.

- With the students, interactively write a response to a literature selection, focusing on one comprehension strategy.

### Procedures
The students will:

- Respond in writing to familiar texts that have been read aloud in class, books that they are currently reading independently, or books used for book clubs.

- Draw a picture, complete a response prompt, or record their thoughts in a journal.

## Beyond the Basic Center

### Additional Center Ideas
- The students write a journal entry, using the voice of a character in a book. Their entries should reflect the character's personality and language structure, as well as events from the story.

- The students respond to literature, using various art media (clay, paint, pastels, colored chalk, collage). They use writing to explain the connection between their artwork and the text.

- The students respond to a text by scripting the

Model for a reading response.

dialogue between characters in a key scene and performing their interpretation as a play. This could be a synthesis of the existing text or an innovation of the theme.

- The students choose a familiar favorite story to map. Included on the story map could be the characters, settings, problems, and solutions.

- Using nonfiction text, the students determine the most important ideas or themes. They then synthesize the information into a poster format with written descriptions justifying the significance of the ideas (photographs with quotes, drawn pictures with slogans, magazine clippings with captions).

Amelia's Recipe for a Journal
1. Take 3 tablespoons of what's on your mind.
2. Stir well and chew it over.
3. Season with descriptions — spice it up!!!
4. Gobble it up! Don't let anyone else see it!

Journaling.

## Additional Resources

Emberly, R. *Three Cool Kids*. Little, Brown & Company, 1995. ISBN 0316236667

Lowell, S. *The Three Little Wolves and the Big Bad Pig*. Simon & Schuster, 1993. ISBN 0689505698

Lowell, S. *The Three Javelinas*. Northland Publishing, 1992. ISBN 0873585429

Marshall, J. *The Three Little Pigs*. Penguin Putnam Books for Young Readers, 2000. ISBN 0448422883

Moss, M. *Amelia's Notebook*. Pleasant Company Publications, 1999. ISBN 1562477870

Moss, M. *Amelia Hits the Road*. Pleasant Company Publications, 1999. ISBN 1562477919

Moss, M. *Amelia Takes Command*. Pleasant Company Publications, 1998. ISBN 1562477897

Wiesner, D. *The Three Pigs*. Houghton Mifflin Company, 2001. ISBN 0618007016

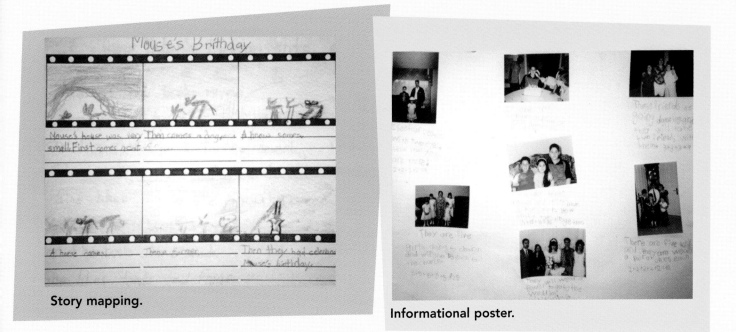

Story mapping.

Informational poster.

# 14. Written Retelling

## Goal
The students will write a retelling of a familiar story.

## Basic Center

### Materials
Paper

Variety of writing tools

Interactively written model of a written retell

Variety of texts

### Preparation
The teacher will:

- Read aloud a text and focus a conversation to retell the events of the story in sequence.

- Facilitate the retelling, using the terms *beginning*, *middle,* and *end.*

- Reread the text and use interactive writing to create a written retelling to post as a model.

## Procedures
The students will:

- Revisit, reread, or listen to a familiar text.

- Retell the text in writing, using pictures or words.

- Include the beginning, middle, and end of the text in the written retelling.

## Beyond the Basic Center

### Additional Center Ideas
- The students choose four events from the story to record in sequence, using pictures and words. They create a "Story Circle" to retell the story to a partner (see pages 156-157). Provide copies of both parts and paper fasteners.

- Provide the students with flannel boards and flannel pieces that are from familiar stories. In a small group, they use flannel pieces and retell the events of the story orally. Then they record their oral retelling in writing.

- Introduce the students to the text structure of a news article during shared reading. Determine the "who," "what," "where," "when," and "why" in the text, and explain that all newspaper articles contain this information. Use interactive writing to retell the events of a familiar story, using the newspaper format. The students then use the format to write their own retellings in the style of a news article.

- Fold a piece of construction paper so that it is has nine squares. While reading a chapter book, the students record a summary of the important events

**A written retell, using *Beginning, Middle*, and *End* with pictures.**

of each chapter in the individual squares. Key events from the chapter may be illustrated beneath the text. Upon completion, they cut apart the squares and have their friends read and sequence the story.

- Introduce the students to story mapping with a graphic organizer. Discuss the elements of a narrative, including setting, characters, problem, story events, and problem resolution. They then use the graphic organizer to plan and organize their written retelling.

## Additional Resources

Babbitt, N. *Tuck Everlasting.* Farrar, Straus and Giroux, 2002. ISBN 0374480133

Blume, J. *Double Fudge.* Penguin Putnam Books for Young Readers, 2002. ISBN 0525469265

Carle, E. *Very Hungry Caterpillar.* Putnam Publishing Group, 1986. ISBN 0399213015

Chabon, W. *Summerland.* Talk Miramax Books, 2002. ISBN 0786808772

Cuyler, M. *100th Day Worries.* Simon & Schuster Books for Young Readers, 2000. ISBN 0689829795

Numeroff, L. *If You Take a Mouse to School.* HarperCollins Children's Books, 2002. ISBN 0060283289

Osbourne, M. *Thanksgiving on Thursday (Magic Tree House #27).* Random House, Inc., 2002. ISBN 0375806156

Park, D. *Junie B., First Grader: Boss of Lunch.* Random House Children's Books, 2002. ISBN 0375815171

Sendak, M. *Where The Wild Things Are.* HarperCollins Children's Books, 1984. ISBN 0064431789

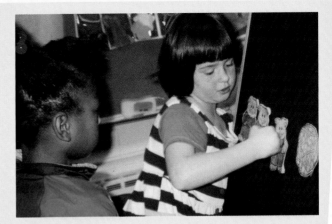

A flannel board retelling.

Learning about questioning skills.

Practicing literary elements.

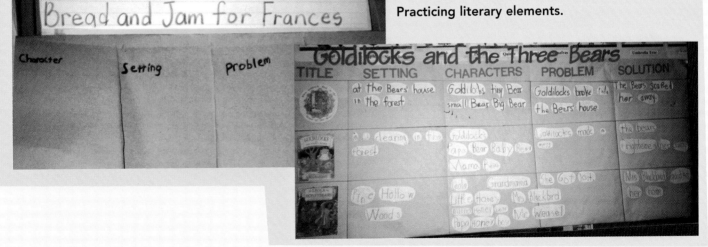

# 15. Presentation

## Goal

The students will demonstrate knowledge about a topic and orally present it to a group.

## Basic Center

### Materials

Collection of artifacts that support a current unit of study

Resource books on the same topic

Paper

Writing tools

### Preparation

The teacher will:

- Collect objects and/or pictures (weather—umbrella, mittens, thermometer; space—rocket, planets, stars; ancient civilizations—mummy, pyramid, hieroglyphics) that represent key understandings of the content area being studied.

- Label the items in the collection, using interactive writing.

- Demonstrate how to use resources to learn more about the topic.

### Procedures

The students will:

- Choose an artifact to research and explain to the group.

- Use resources to review and learn additional information about the artifact.

- Write notes, using key words to plan for an oral presentation.

- Orally present the information to a group, using the artifact as a prop.

## Beyond the Basic Center

### Additional Center Ideas

- After the guided reading lesson, help the students to orally retell the story, focusing on sequencing and using beginning, middle, and end. Provide strips of transparency film, overhead markers, and a tag board window. The students use the window to trace three boxes, left to right, on the transparency film. They choose a story to illustrate on the transparency, showing the beginning, middle, and end. Then they retell the story by sliding the tag board window, framing each picture, while orally retelling the story one scene at a time.

- Read aloud and share read a variety of Mother Goose rhymes. Provide opportunities to use props in acting out the poems as they are being recited. The students choose a rhyme to perform and write a list of needed materials. Then they create props, practice their performance, and orally present the poems for a group.

Presenting information orally.

Orally presenting in a group.

- Interactively write a class rubric for oral presentations. The students practice an oral presentation with a partner, who scores the presentation using the rubric and writes comments and suggestions for improvement.

- Use interactive editing to change a narrative text to a script. The students then use this process to create their own scripts from familiar texts. They create puppets and props to accompany their oral presentation of their play.

- As a culminating activity, the students work in groups to demonstrate their understanding of key concepts. They review information learned during a content area study and choose a format (news broadcast, commercial, documentary) for a video presentation. The students work together to write a script, assign parts, develop props, and orally present information. Completed videos may be shown to the class or shared with parents.

Performing interactively edited text.

## Additional Resources

Brandley, F. *International Space Station*. HarperCollins Children's Books, 2000. ISBN 0064452093

Ganeri, A. *Earth & Space: A Question and Answer Book*. Barnes & Noble Books, 2000. ISBN 0760734240

Gribbin, M. *Eyewitness: Time and Space*. DK Publishing, Inc., 2000. ISBN 0789455781

Martin, J. *Snowflake Bentley*. Houghton Mifflin Company, 1998. ISBN 0395861624

Putnam, J. *Amazing Facts About Ancient Egypt*. Harry N. Abrams, Inc., 1994. ISBN 0810919532

Scieszka, J. *See You Later, Gladiator*. Penguin Putnam Books for Young Readers, 2000. ISBN 1402870094

Simon, S. *Weather*. HarperCollins Children's Books, 2000. ISBN 0439102758

White, W. *The Magic School Bus Kicks Up a Storm: A Book About Weather*. Scholastic, Inc., 2000. ISBN 0439102758

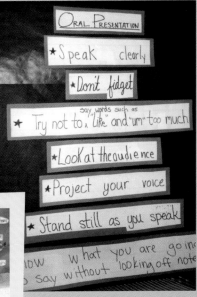

Oral presentation rubric.

Culminating group activity.

# 16. Create a Story

## Goal

The students will practice writing a narrative that describes an event or experience.

## Basic Center

### Materials

Variety of writing tools

Paper

### Preparation

The teacher will:

- Use interactive writing to describe a common experience. Teaching points will include choosing a topic, maintaining a focus, and logical sequencing of events.

- Have an accessible display of interactive writing that the students can use as a resource.

### Procedures

The students will:

- Write narratives based on events or personal experiences.

- Read their narrative to a friend in order to receive feedback for revision and editing.

- Participate in a "Super Writer" small group by reading aloud and sharing completed narratives.

## Beyond the Basic Center

### Additional Center Ideas

- Collect an assortment of wordless books and a variety of post-it notes in different sizes. The students write text on the post-it notes that narrate the story depicted in the illustrations. Then they share the story with a friend.

- Label containers with story elements (setting, characters, problem, solution, details). Label tongue depressors with several ideas from each category (setting: cottage, deserted island, pyramids of ancient Egypt) and place them in the appropriate containers. The students choose one or more tongue depressor(s) from each container in order to compose a narrative.

- Collect photographs from a variety of sources (magazines, calendars, postcards) and place them in a container. The students select a picture and write a narrative describing the event or experience depicted.

- As a class, decorate a "Memory Backpack." Throughout the year collect artifacts that represent academic and social learning and place them in the backpack. The students choose artifact(s) from the backpack and write a narrative describing why the selected event or experience was memorable.

- Collect a variety of comic strips that have multiple frames. The students choose a comic strip to rewrite as a story. They are encouraged to include the narrative device of dialogue.

Writing to a friend.

Organizing for a writing center.

## Additional Resources

Bunting, E. *The Memory String*. Houghton Mifflin Company, 2000.
ISBN 0395861462

Clarke, C. *The Night Before Christmas*. Little, Brown & Company, 2002.
ISBN 0316832715

Delton, J. *A Big Box of Memories*. Random House Children's Books, 2000.
ISBN 0440415284

Fletcher, C. *The Adventures of Tom Sawyer*. Kingfisher, 2002. ISBN 0753454785

Fox, M. *Wilfred Gordon McDonald Partridge*. Kane/Miller Book Publishers, 1991. ISBN 091629126X

Polacco, P. *Thank You Mr. Falker*. Putnam Publishing, 1998. ISBN 0399231668

Williams, M. *The Velveteen Rabbit*. Troll Communications, 2002. ISBN 0816752826

**Using a variety of resources to locate information for writing.**

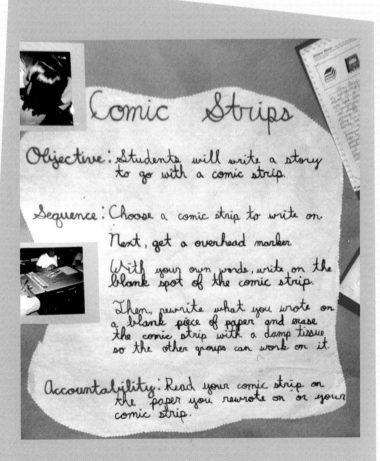

**Rewriting comic strips.**

# 17. Content Area

## Goal

The students will write to communicate their understandings in the content areas.

## Basic Center

### Materials

Journals

Writing tools

### Preparation

The teacher will:

- Read aloud from a content area text and then engage the students in an interactive writing lesson responding to the text.

- Display some interactive writing as a reference to be used in the literacy center.

- Collect and organize an assortment of texts related to the current unit of study. These will be for student use.

### Procedures

The students will:

- Select a text of interest to read.

- Write or draw a response to the information in the text, using their journal (summary, fact-question-response, reactions, new learning).

## Beyond the Basic Center

### Additional Center Ideas

- Choose a classroom mascot. Interactively write a postcard that explains how the mascot travels to various locations to deliver information. Referencing the interactively written postcard, the students design and write their own postcards (see Page 150), summarizing information learned during a content area of study. Send the completed postcards, mascot, and explanation to someone who will respond (students in other classrooms, the principal, members of the city council).

- The students write diary entries detailing their understandings about the current unit of study. They may write from their own perspective or from the point of view of a content area figure or object (community worker, farmer, seed, microscope).

- Choose a variety of short texts related to the current unit of study. The students identify the important content area words that convey the meaning of the text. Next, they use these words to create various types of poems (acrostic, cinquain, haiku).

- The students use a time line to sequence events. They compile information from a variety of content area texts. Then they determine and organize the key events in order to label the time line (title, dates, events with descriptions). Appropriate graphics

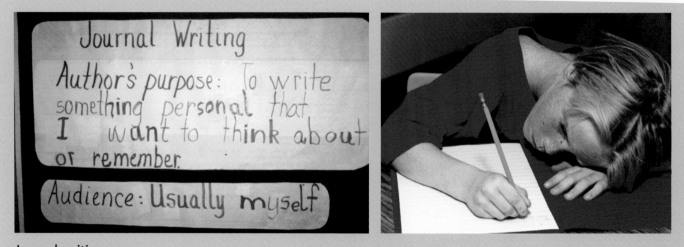

Journal writing.

**Interactively written postcard.**

**Examples of diaries.**

should be added (student illustrations, magazine pictures, computer clip art).

- With a partner, the students gather information from a variety of content area resources in order to create a PowerPoint presentation. They will choose information to include in their presentation. They organize their information by topic, write appropriate headings, and select graphics or special effects. Then they rehearse their presentation and present it to the class.

### Additional Resources

Hopkinson, D. *Sweet Clara and the Freedom Quilt.* Alfred A. Knopf, 1995. ISBN 0679874720

Kalman, B. *Community Workers From A-Z.* Crabtree Publishing Company, 1997. ISBN 0865054045

Kramer, S. *Hidden Worlds: Looking Through a Scientist's Microscope.* Houghton Mifflin Company, 2001. ISBN 0618055460

Moss, M. *Amelia Lends a Hand.* Pleasant Company Publications, 2002. ISBN 1584855398

Moss, M. *Amelia's School Survival Guide.* Pleasant Company Publications, 2002. ISBN 1584855096

Polacco, P. *Pink and Say.* Putnam Publishing Group, 1994. ISBN 0399226710

Saunders-Smith, G. *Communities.* Capstone Press, 1997. ISBN 1560654945

Silverstein, A. *A World in a Drop of Water: Exploring with a Microscope.* Dover Publications Inc., 1998. ISBN 0486403815

**Sequence of events using a time line.**

# Assessment

The assessments provided here are directed primarily at informing teaching. Teaching can be both more effective and efficient when the teacher has information about what the student knows and has control of and where the student needs continued teacher support.

### Literacy Skills Checklist

The Literacy Skills Checklist is provided as a resource for teachers to record skill acquisition for each student. This checklist is not designed to be used as a test. The source of information for the checklist is the teacher's observation of reading and writing behaviors in classroom activities. There is no regular order in which students will exhibit these skills.

### Record of Oral Reading

The Record of Oral Reading is designed to record student behaviors during guided reading. Errors made by students, comprehension probes, corrections, accuracy, and fluency are all recorded. This information is used to guide book selections for future reading and to use individual student reading behaviors to inform instruction.

### Observation Guide

The Observation Guide is a form that can be used to record teacher observations during various teaching activities. The record is anecdotal and includes both student behaviors and teacher prompts.

### Guided Reading Procedures and Self-Assessment

The procedural checklist and self-assessment are used to plan guided reading and follow-up activities. This checklist supports decision making for teachers before, during, and after the guided reading.

# Literacy Skills Checklist

The Literacy Skills Checklist is provided as a resource for teachers to record skill acquisition for each student. This checklist is not designed to be used as a test. The source of this information is the teacher's observation of reading and writing behaviors in classroom activities. There is no regular order in which students will exhibit these skills.

When using this checklist with older students, use only the skill level that applies to the students at their grade level.

## Alphabet

*NOTE: Assess the student's ability to recognize, locate, and name letters prior to instruction so that you can tailor your teaching to each student's needs.*

Recognizes and names letters *(Circle those the student knows.)*

| a | b | c | d | e | f | g | h | i | j | k | l | m | n | o | p | q | r | s | t | u | v | w | x | y | z |
| A | B | C | D | E | F | G | H | I | J | K | L | M | N | O | P | Q | R | S | T | U | V | W | X | Y | Z |

Sings or recites the alphabet (with or without a model)

## Phonemic Awareness *(Check when demonstrated.)*

☐ Claps syllables in words
☐ Counts syllables in multi-syllabic words
☐ Recognizes rhymes
☐ Produces rhyme
☐ Blends segmented sounds to say words
☐ Blends different beginning sounds with phonograms (onset and rime)
☐ Segments sounds in monosyllabic words
☐ Manipulates sounds by substituting one sound for another
☐ Manipulates sounds by adding or subtracting one sound

## Phonics

Associates alphabet letters with these basic sounds
*(Circle those the student knows.)*

| b/b/ | c/k/s/ | d/d/ | f/f/ | g/g/j/ | h/h/ |
| j/j/ | k/k/ | l/l/ | m/m/ | n/n/ | p/p/ |
| q/kw/ | r/r/ | s/s/ | t/t/ | v/v/ | w/w/ |
| x/ks/ | y/y/ | z/z/ | | | |

Recognizes short vowel sounds *(Circle those the student knows.)*
/ă/   /ĕ/   /ĭ/   /ŏ/   /ŭ/

Recognizes long vowel sounds *(Circle those the student knows.)*
/ā/   /ē/   /ī/   /ō/   /ū/

Reads and locates words with these vowel letter-sound correspondences
*(Circle those the student regularly decodes in words.)*

| | | | | |
|---|---|---|---|---|
| *ai* as in *wait* | *ee* as in *need* | *oo* as in *moon* | *ou* as in *though* | *ir* as in *fir* |
| *ay* as in *day* | *oa* as in *goat* | *oo* as in *look* | *ou* as in *loud* | *ur* as in *hurt* |
| *ea* as in *beat* | *ow* as in *how* | *oi* as in *boil* | *ou* as in *youth* | *ar* as in *cart* |
| *ea* as in *head* | *ow* as in *grow* | *oy* as in *boy* | *er* as in *her* | *or* as in *fort* |

Recognizes alternative sounds of consonant letters
*(Circle those the student knows.)*

| | | | |
|---|---|---|---|
| *c* as in *cat* | *g* as in *giraffe* | *ch* as in *chef* | *th* as in *through* |
| *c* as in *circus* | *ch* as in *Christmas* | *sh* as in *shoe* | *wh* as in *what* |
| *g* as in *gate* | *ch* as in *church* | *th* as in *that* | *wh* as in *who* |

Reads and locates words with these initial consonant blends
*(Circle those the student knows.)*

| | | | | | | | |
|---|---|---|---|---|---|---|---|
| br | cr | dr | fr | gr | pr | tr | wr |
| bl | cl | fl | gl | pl | sl | | |
| sc | sk | sm | sn | sp | st | sw | |
| scr | squ | str | spr | spl | shr | sch | |
| dw | tw | thr | | | | | |

Reads and locates words with these final consonant blends
*(Circle those the student knows.)*

| | | | | | | |
|---|---|---|---|---|---|---|
| ct | ft | lt | nt | pt | rt | st |
| ld | nd | rd | nk | sk | mp | nc(e) |

**Print Awareness** *(Check when demonstrated.)*
- ☐ Locates the front of a book
- ☐ Recognizes that print is what is read on a page
- ☐ Can point out where text begins
- ☐ Follows a line of print from left to right
- ☐ Moves from right-hand end of one line to left-hand beginning of next
- ☐ Points to each word as it is read
- ☐ Recognizes when sentences begin and end
- ☐ Understands that a question mark indicates a sentence asks a question
- ☐ Understands that an exclamation mark indicates the sentence should be read with excitement or surprise
- ☐ Understands that quotation marks come before and after words said by a character

## Reading Skills

Reads and locates high frequency words *(Circle those the student recognizes with regularity.)*

| | | | | | |
|---|---|---|---|---|---|
| a | about | all | an | and | are |
| as | at | be | been | but | by |
| call | can | come | could | day | did |
| do | down | each | find | first | for |
| from | get | go | had | has | have |
| he | her | him | his | how | I |
| if | in | into | is | it | its |
| like | long | look | made | make | many |
| may | more | my | no | not | now |
| number | of | oil | on | one | or |
| other | out | part | people | said | see |
| she | so | some | than | that | the |
| their | them | then | there | these | they |
| this | time | to | two | up | use |
| was | water | way | we | were | what |
| when | which | who | will | with | word |
| would | write | you | your | | |

*(Check when demonstrated.)*

- ☐ Reads and locates words with short *a*, as in *cap*
- ☐ Reads and locates words with short *e*, as in *bed*
- ☐ Reads and locates words with short *i, as in trip*
- ☐ Reads and locates words with short *o*, as in *box*
- ☐ Reads and locates words with short *u*, as in *rug*
- ☐ Reads and locates words with long *a*
  - ☐ spelled *a* as in *paper*
  - ☐ spelled *a*-consonant-*e* as in *game*
  - ☐ spelled *ai* as in *rain*
  - ☐ spelled *ay* as in *play*
- ☐ Reads and locates words with long *e*
  - ☐ spelled *ea* as in *eat*
  - ☐ spelled *ee* as in *feed*
  - ☐ spelled *e*-consonant-*e* as in *delete*
  - ☐ spelled *e* as in *he*
  - ☐ spelled *eo* as in *people*
  - ☐ spelled *ie* as in *believe*
  - ☐ spelled *ei* as in *receive*

- ☐ Reads and locates words with long *i*
  - ☐ spelled *i* as in *hi*
  - ☐ spelled *ie* as in *tried*
  - ☐ spelled *y* as in *my*
  - ☐ spelled *i*-consonant-*e* as in *ice*
  - ☐ spelled *igh* as in *right*
- ☐ Reads and locates words with long *o*
  - ☐ spelled *o*-consonant-*e* as in *home*
  - ☐ spelled *oa* as in *road*
  - ☐ spelled *ow* as in *mow*
  - ☐ spelled *oe* as in *toe*
  - ☐ spelled *o* as in *go*
  - ☐ spelled *oh*
- ☐ Reads and locates words with long *u*
  - ☐ spelled *u*-consonant-*e* as in *tune*
  - ☐ spelled *ue* as in *Tuesday*
  - ☐ spelled *u* as in *music*
  - ☐ spelled *eau* as in *beautiful*
  - ☐ spelled *oo* as in *noon*
  - ☐ spelled *ou* as in *youth*
  - ☐ spelled *o* as in *who*

**Reading Behaviors** *(Check when demonstrated.)*
- ☐ Directionality
- ☐ One-to-one matching
- ☐ Return sweep
- ☐ Concept of first and last part of word, sentence, story
- ☐ Locating known and unknown words
- ☐ Comparing sources of information
- ☐ Fluency

**Written Language and Concept Development**
*(Check those the student recognizes, locates, reads, and writes.)*
- ☐ Punctuation
- ☐ Spelling and word analysis
- ☐ Sentence structure
- ☐ Grammar
- ☐ Parts of speech
- ☐ Irregular words
- ☐ Contractions
- ☐ Antonyms
- ☐ Synonyms
- ☐ Homographs
- ☐ Homophones
- ☐ Metaphors
- ☐ Similes
- ☐ Idioms

**Comprehension**
*Structural Features of Informational Materials*
*(Check those the student is able to recognize, locate, and read.)*
- ☐ Title
- ☐ Table of contents
- ☐ Author
- ☐ Illustrator
- ☐ Chapter headings
- ☐ Glossary
- ☐ Index

*(Check those the student is able to read and interpret.)*
- ☐ Information from diagrams, charts, captions, and graphs
- ☐ Sequence, chronological order
- ☐ Cause and effect
- ☐ Fact and opinion

## Structural Features of Literary Materials

*(Check those the student is able to read and interpret.)*

☐ Styles of literature (including poetry, drama, fiction, nonfiction, fantasies, fables, myths, legends, and fairy tales)

☐ Strategies of reading for different purposes

☐ Sequence

☐ Figurative language

☐ Sentence structure

☐ Rhythm

## Comprehension and Analysis

*(Check those the student is able to recognize, locate, and use.)*

☐ Pictures, context, captions, charts, maps, and graphs, to determine unknown words and make predictions

☐ Confirm or discount predictions in order to make new predictions or modify predictions

☐ *Who, What, When, Where, Why,* and *How* questions

☐ Written directions (e.g., one step, two step, multiple steps)

☐ Key words

☐ Clarifying questions

☐ Restate facts and details

☐ Connect to life experiences

☐ Relate prior knowledge to text

☐ Retell familiar stories, expository, narrative passages

☐ Inferences

☐ Main idea and supporting details

## Narrative Analysis

*(Check those the student is able to recognize and read.)*

☐ Fantasy versus reality

☐ Types of everyday print

☐ Plot, character, setting, and important events

☐ Theme or moral in a selected text

☐ Author's purpose

☐ Identify the speaker and recognize the difference between first and third person narration

# 7. **Record of Oral Reading**

Student Name _____ Date _____

Recorder _____

Name of Book/Text _____

Level (if known) _____ Fiction _____ Nonfiction_____

## During the Reading

1.  Record each error in the first column. Write what the student *read* over the *actual word* in the text.

    Example:   said
              ―――
               say

2.  In the second and third columns, check the sources of information the student was trying to use.
    Phonics: Was the student trying to use letter-sound information to decode the word?
    Comprehension: Was the student trying to use the meaning of the text to determine the word?

If the student corrects an error, place a C beside the error that was corrected.

| Errors | Phonics ✔ | Comprehension ✔ |
|---|---|---|
|  |  |  |

## Scoring

### 1. *Comprehension Probes* *(Choose a minimum of two probes. Notate confusions.)*

Did this story end the way you thought it would? How was it different?

What questions do you still have about this text?

What did you learn from this text?

What might you have done if you were a character in this story?

Did this story remind you of something that has happened to you or to someone you know?

*Record your overall impression of student comprehension.*    *Adequate* ☐    *Inadequate* ☐

### 2. *Corrections*

How many corrections did the student make during the reading? _____

What sources of information were used for these corrections? Record number.

Phonics _____        Comprehension _____

### 3. Accuracy

Number of words read _____ minus errors _____ = words correct

$$\frac{\text{Words correct}}{\text{Words read}} = \frac{\rule{2cm}{0.4pt}}{\text{\% Accuracy}}$$

95-100% Accuracy—Easy reading level

90-95% Accuracy—Instructional reading level

90% Accuracy or less—Frustration reading level

### 4. Fluency

*Record your overall impression of student fluency* _____

4—High: Phrased and fluent most of the time; problem solving is rapid.

3—Some phrased reading, with obvious problem solving and rereading.

2—Word-by-word reading; inconsistent attention to phonics and comprehension.

1—Low: Frequent pausing; mostly word-by-word reading; slow problem solving.

### 5. Overall Impressions

What strengths and needs were observed for this student?

_____

_____

### 6. Planning

Impact of this observation on:

Book selection _____

Instruction _____

# Observation Guide

Student Name _____ Date _____

Notate student behaviors and teacher prompts.

| Reading Aloud | Guided Reading/Reciprocal Teaching/ Book Clubs |
|---|---|
| | |
| **Shared Reading** | **Independent Reading** |
| | |
| **Interactive Writing/Interactive Editing** | **Independent Writing** |
| | |

Summary – Implications for instruction: _____

_____

_____

_____

# 9. Guided Reading Procedures and Self-Assessment

## Planning for the Guided Reading

### Management:  Literacy Centers

Are students familiar with the procedures, expectations and have materials for all literacy centers?

_____

Are all students able to successfully complete the planned literacy centers?

_____

Are the literacy centers multileveled for all students to work at an independent level?

_____

### Management:  Reading Groups

How will I decide on group membership?  ✔ Check all that apply.

☐  Text Reading Level  (Record of Oral Reading, Literacy Skills Checklist, Observation Guide)

☐  Sources of Information (phonics, comprehension)

☐  Oral Reading Behaviors (monitoring, comparing sources of information, fluency, correction)

☐  Comprehension Strategies

☐  Interest

### Materials

How will I choose text for each group?  ✔ Check all that apply.

☐  Sentence/Book Length

☐  Vocabulary and Language Structure

☐  Text Layout and Picture Support

☐  Text Type and Subject Matter

☐  Word Analysis Skills

Do I have the text I need for each group?  Do I have enough copies for each student in the group?

Group:_____ Title:_____Level:_____ Number of Copies:_____

Group:_____ Title:_____Level:_____ Number of Copies:_____

Group:_____ Title:_____Level:_____ Number of Copies:_____

Group:_____ Title:_____Level:_____ Number of Copies:_____

Group:_____ Title:_____Level:_____ Number of Copies:_____

# Before the Guided Reading
## Book Introduction

Consider each of the following for every reading group.

When I read the text do I keep my students' strengths and needs in mind?

_____

What information do students need to read this text successfully?

_____

Have I prepared an introduction that will encourage students to discuss what this text will be about?

_____

What are my purposes for using this text with students?

_____

What will I say to encourage conversation in order for students to relate new information to what they already know?

_____

What parts of the introduction will I need to focus on and emphasize?

_____

Based on my observation of students what will I include in my book introduction?
✔ Check all that apply.

☐ Address individual reading needs          ☐ Meaning

☐ Book Language          ☐ Text and Print Features

☐ Text Organization          ☐ Reading Behaviors

☐ Comprehension Strategies          ☐ Story Elements

☐ Vocabulary          ☐ Content and Standards

☐ Interest

# During the Guided Reading

Is every student reading orally?

_____

Am I listening to every student read?

_____

What did I notice about each student's reading behavior?  ✔ Check all that apply.
*Is the student:*

☐ Attending to print and text features          ☐ Comparing sources of information

☐ Monitoring                                                  ☐ Fluent

☐ Correcting                                                  ☐ Confident

☐ Using sources of information (phonics, comprehension)

Did I use appropriate prompts to support reading strategies?

_____

Did I record what I observed about students' reading behavior?

_____


## After the Guided Reading

### Discussing Text

Did I provide the opportunity to discuss the text following the reading?

_____

If so, what focus did the text discussion have?  ✔ Check all that apply.

☐ Questioning                    ☐ Connections

☐ Retelling                        ☐ Language Structure

☐ Text and Print Features     ☐ Vocabulary

How did I provide opportunities for rereading the text independently and in small groups?

_____

Will students independently complete book extension activities in literacy centers?
✔ Check all that apply.

☐ Phonics                          ☐ Phonemic Awareness

☐ Vocabulary                     ☐ Fluency

☐ Text Comprehension        ☐ Writing

## Planning: Next Lessons

*Based on today's lesson:*

What did students learn?

_____

What new learning should be reinforced or extended?

_____

Are students grouped appropriately?

_____

Did the book introduction provide the appropriate level of support?

_____

What book should this group read next?

_____

How will I use my anecdotal notes to plan for the next guided reading lesson?

_____


## Management: Literacy Centers

*Based on today's lesson:*

Did the literacy centers provide opportunities for reading, writing, and skill application?

_____

Was each literacy center engaging for students?

_____

Were students able to independently participate in activities?

_____

Were there literacy centers that need review of procedures and expectations?

_____

# Appendices

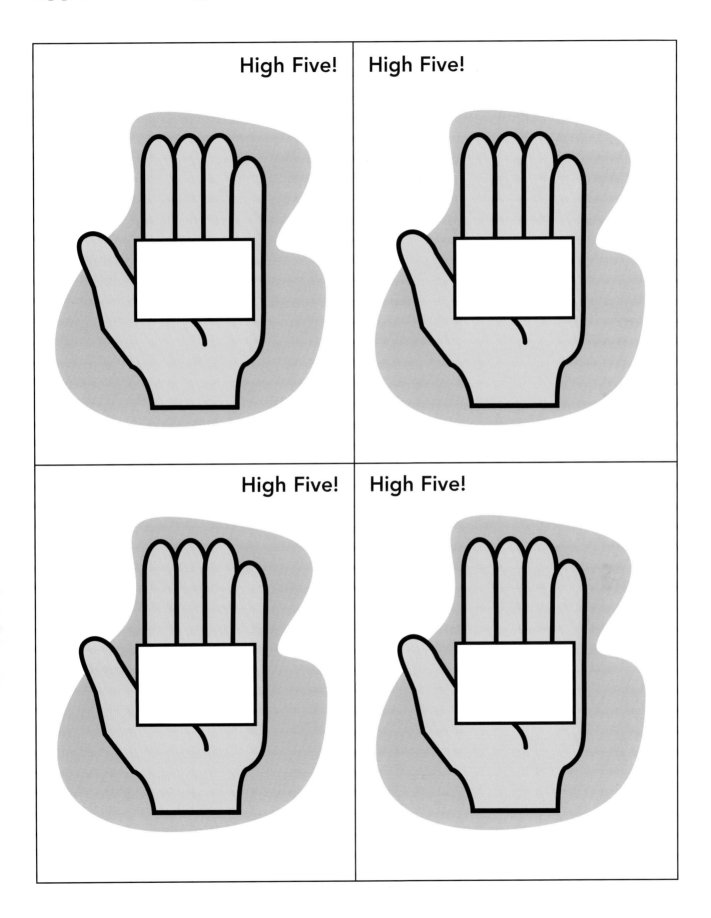

High Five! High Five!

High Five! High Five!

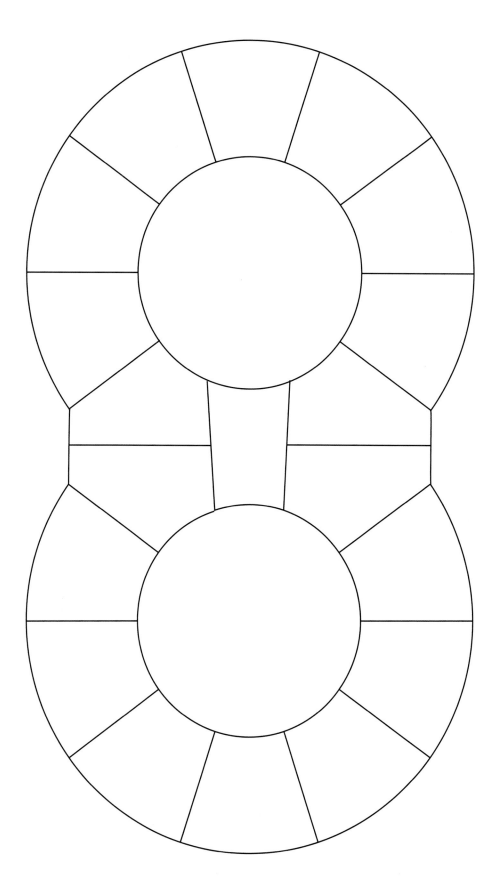

## Appendix 3 • Counting Syllables

| 1 Syllable | 2 Syllables | 3 Syllables | More |
|---|---|---|---|
|  |  |  |  |

To: _____

Date: _____ Time: _____

### WHILE YOU WERE OUT

M _____

Of _____

_____

Phone: _____

      Area Code     Number     Extension

☐ Telephoned    ☐ Wants To See You

☐ Please Call      ☐ Urgent

☐ Called To See You  ☐ Returned Your Call

☐ Will Call Again

Message _____

_____

Message Taken By

_____

---

To: _____

Date: _____ Time: _____

### WHILE YOU WERE OUT

M _____

Of _____

_____

Phone: _____

      Area Code     Number     Extension

☐ Telephoned    ☐ Wants To See You

☐ Please Call      ☐ Urgent

☐ Called To See You  ☐ Returned Your Call

☐ Will Call Again

Message _____

_____

Message Taken By

_____

---

To: _____

Date: _____ Time: _____

### WHILE YOU WERE OUT

M _____

Of _____

_____

Phone: _____

      Area Code     Number     Extension

☐ Telephoned    ☐ Wants To See You

☐ Please Call      ☐ Urgent

☐ Called To See You  ☐ Returned Your Call

☐ Will Call Again

Message _____

_____

Message Taken By

_____

---

To: _____

Date: _____ Time: _____

### WHILE YOU WERE OUT

M _____

Of _____

_____

Phone: _____

      Area Code     Number     Extension

☐ Telephoned    ☐ Wants To See You

☐ Please Call      ☐ Urgent

☐ Called To See You  ☐ Returned Your Call

☐ Will Call Again

Message _____

_____

Message Taken By

_____

# Appendix 5 • Fluency Chart

| Title | Time in Seconds | | | |
| | 1st Reading | 2nd Reading | 3rd Reading | 4th Reading |
|---|---|---|---|---|
| | | | | |
| | | | | |
| | | | | |
| | | | | |
| | | | | |
| | | | | |
| | | | | |
| | | | | |
| | | | | |
| | | | | |
| | | | | |
| | | | | |
| | | | | |
| | | | | |
| | | | | |
| | | | | |
| | | | | |
| | | | | |
| | | | | |
| | | | | |
| | | | | |
| | | | | |
| | | | | |

Place
Stamp
Here

Place
Stamp
Here

## Appendix 8 · Dictionary Recording Sheet

| Entry Word | Guide Words | Time |
|---|---|---|
|  |  |  |
|  |  |  |
|  |  |  |
|  |  |  |
|  |  |  |
|  |  |  |
|  |  |  |
|  |  |  |
|  |  |  |
|  |  |  |
|  |  |  |
|  |  |  |
|  |  |  |
|  |  |  |
|  |  |  |
|  |  |  |
|  |  |  |
|  |  |  |
|  |  |  |
|  |  |  |
|  |  |  |
|  |  |  |
|  |  |  |
|  |  |  |
|  |  |  |
|  |  |  |
|  |  |  |
|  |  |  |
|  |  |  |
|  |  |  |

# Appendix 9 • Web Organizer

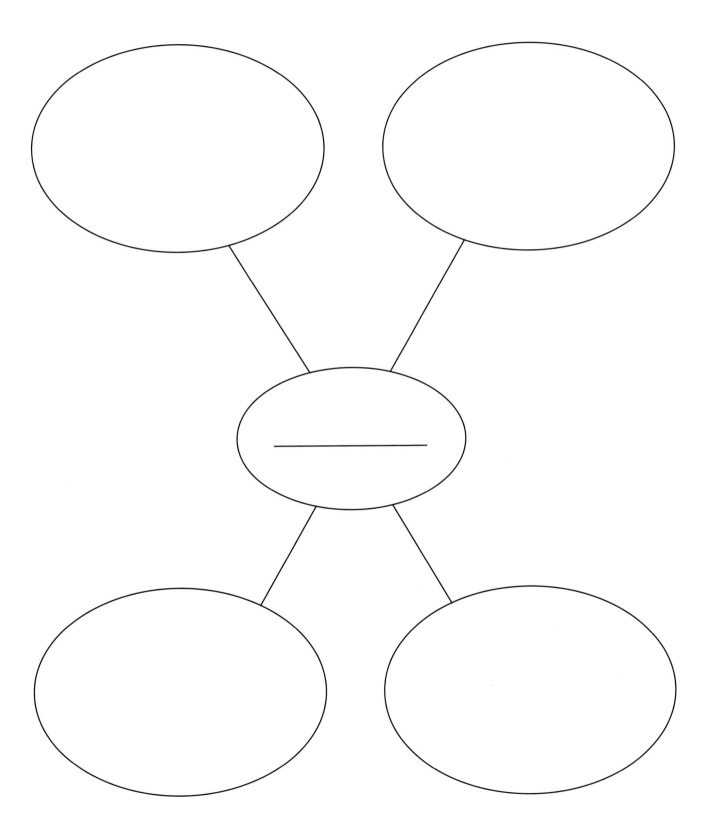

Name _____ Date _____

# All Sorts of Words

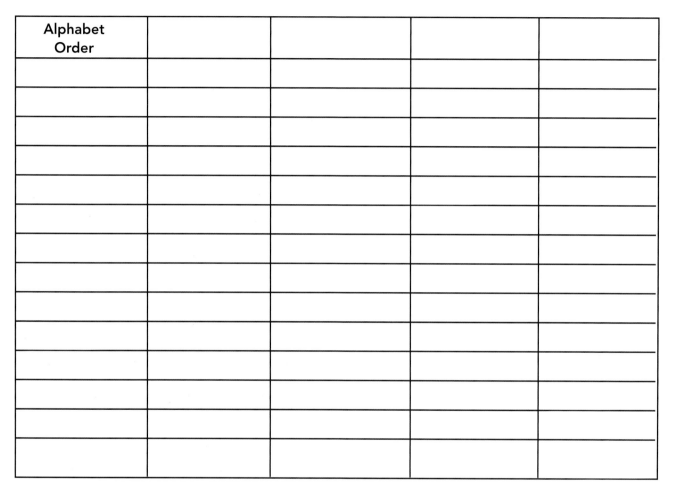

| Alphabet Order | | | | |
|---|---|---|---|---|
| | | | | |
| | | | | |
| | | | | |
| | | | | |
| | | | | |
| | | | | |
| | | | | |
| | | | | |
| | | | | |
| | | | | |
| | | | | |
| | | | | |
| | | | | |

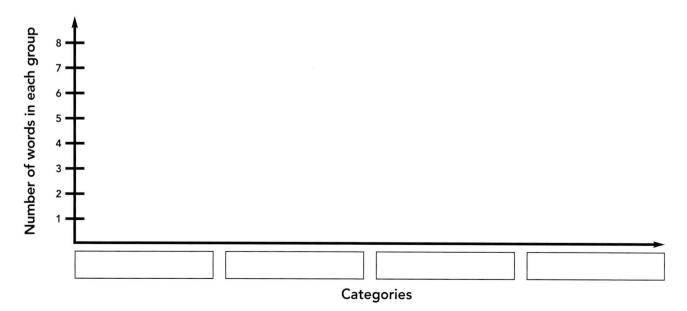

Number of words in each group

8
7
6
5
4
3
2
1

Categories

# Appendix 11 • The Fry Readability Graph

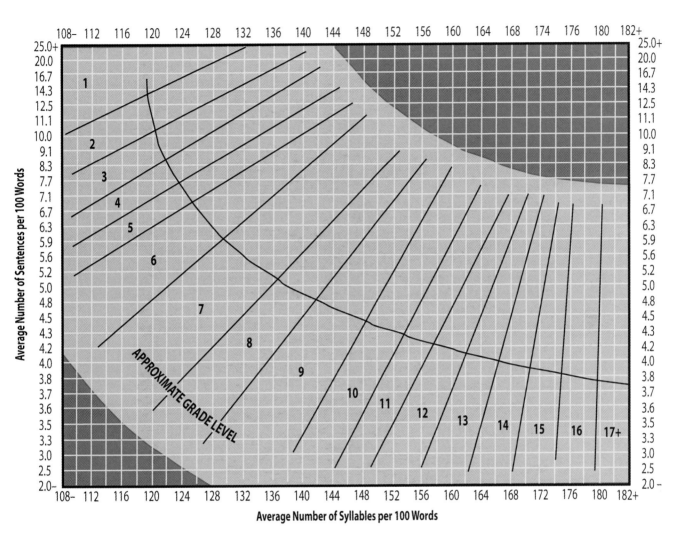

**FIGURE 4.2** The Fry readability graph. From *Journal of Reading, 21, 242 – 252*

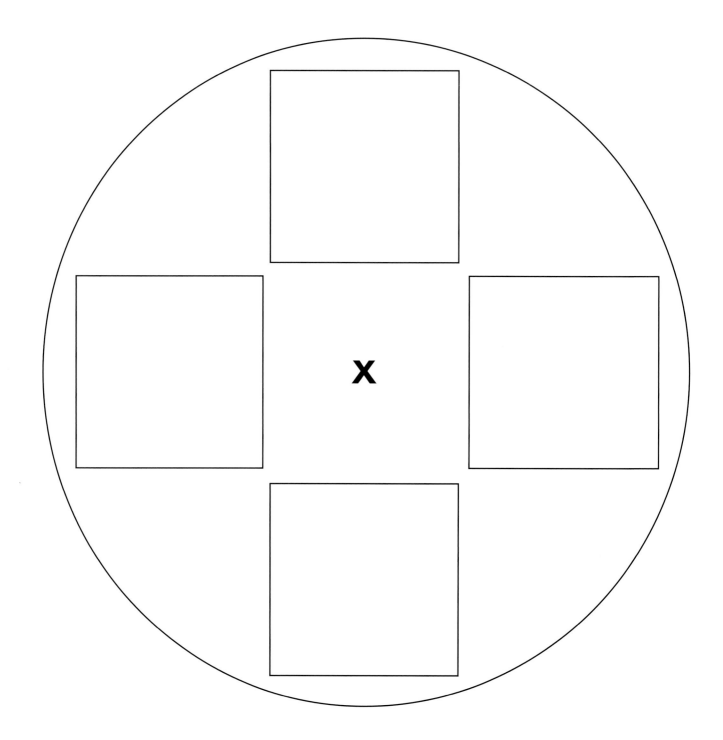

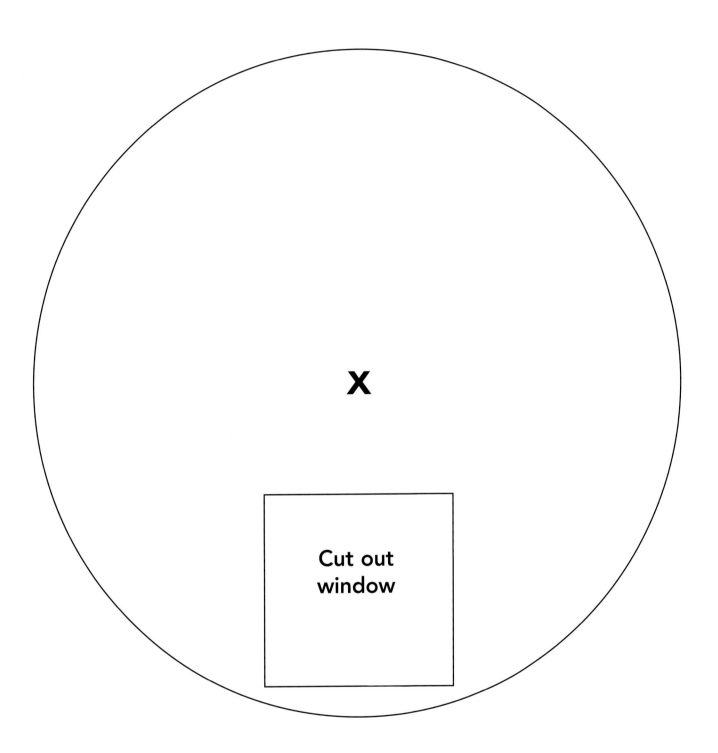

X

Cut out
window

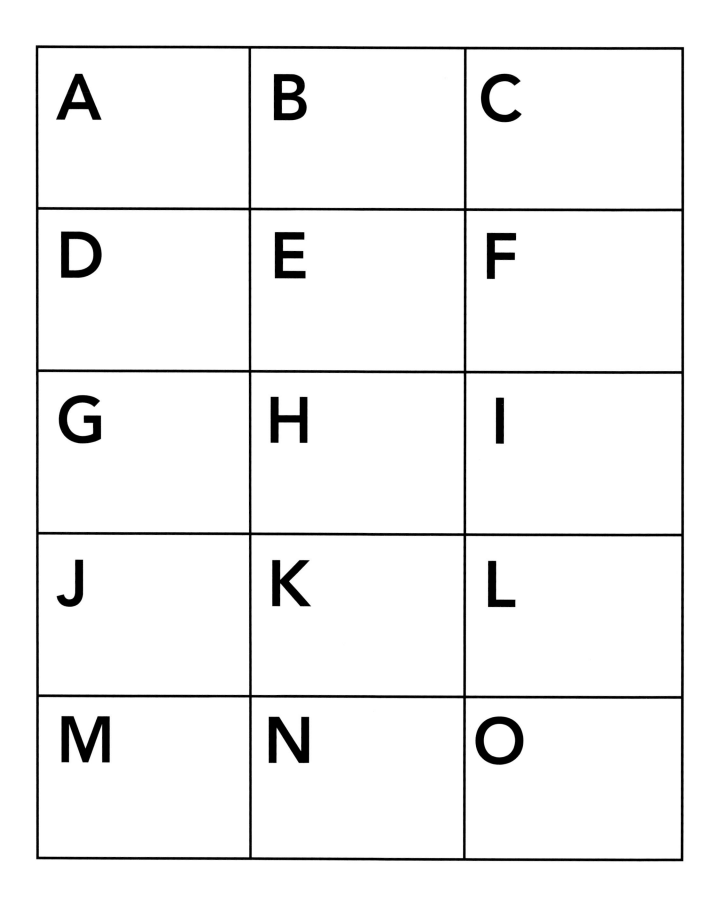

| | | |
|---|---|---|
| P | Q | R |
| S | T | U |
| V | W | X |
| Y | Z | |

# Glossary

**Acrostic.** A puzzle in which particular letters spell a word

**Adjective.** A part of speech that modifies a noun

**Adverb.** The part of speech that modifies a verb, adjective, or another adverb

**Alliteration.** Repetition of initial sounds in several words or in a phrase

**Alphabetic principle.** The concept underlying writing systems that each phoneme/sound should have its own grapheme/letter

**Anthology.** A collection of text pieces, including fiction, nonfiction, and poetry

**Artifacts.** Student products from a lesson, usually in writing, that students can refer to and use in other work in the classroom

**Assessment.** Data gathered in order to understand the strengths and needs of a student; data can include observations, formal and informal testing, surveys, and samples of student work

**Background knowledge.** Information that readers and writers bring to a task, based on what they already know or have experienced

**Bar graph.** A chart representing data frequency using parallel rectangular bars

**Blends.** Joining of sounds represented by two or more letters with minimal changes in those sounds

**Book club.** An instructional grouping that is used for students to read, discuss, and write about a book at their ability and interest levels

**Characters.** Persons in a story or drama

**Cinquain.** A stanza of five lines with the lines having the order of two, four, six, eight, and two syllables

**Clip art.** Pictures in the public domain from software or websites

**Collaborative model.** A method for special and regular teachers to plan and teach together in the regular classroom

**Concepts of print.** Basic elements of reading, including book handling, directionality, reading the punctuation, recognizing letters and words, and matching sound to letter

**Connections.** Relating to a text by linking what readers bring from themselves and their feelings, from other texts, and from their experiences in the world

**Correction.** When a reader or writer notices an error and corrects it without assistance

**Decode.** To analyze spoken or written symbols of a language in order to understand the intended meaning

**Derivatives.** Words formed by adding an affix to the root word

**Digraphs.** Two letters that represent one speech sound

**Diphthong.** A single vowel sound made from two vowels together in a syllable

**Disabilities.** Learning and behavior problems that affect learning and qualify students for special education

**English language learners.** A designation (ELL) used for students who speak a primary language other than English when the language of classroom instruction is English

**Fiction**. A form of literature that is not true

**Figurative language**. The use of various figures of speech such as metaphors or similes

**Fluency**. The ability to read quickly and accurately

**Format**. Features of text layout on a page or in a book

**Frustration reading level**. Text that is too difficult to decode and comprehend; usually at the 90% level or below, based on readability formulas or leveling of texts

**Graphic organizer**. A visual outline or representational tool for planning a piece of writing or an oral presentation

**Guided reading**. A teaching method in which students read orally and the teacher provides direct instruction in phonics and comprehension

**Haiku**. A type of poetry consisting of seventeen syllables and three lines

**High frequency words**. Words that occur very often in spoken or written language

**Idiomatic expression**. A unique meaning used by a group of people

**Inclusion**. The philosophy and practice of providing special education services for students with disabilities in the regular classroom

**Independent reading**. A teaching method that allows students to practice strategies being learned, develops fluency, and encourages successful problem solving

**Independent reading level**. Text that is decoded and comprehended for independent work by the student; usually at the 95% level or above, based on readability formulas or leveling of texts

**Independent writing**. A teaching method that encourages writing for different purposes and audiences and the fostering of creativity in writing

**Informational text**. A type of nonfiction text with the purpose of explanation of material

**Instructional reading level**. Text that is able to be decoded and comprehended for instructional work by the child; usually at the 90-95% level, based on readability formulas or leveling of texts

**Interactive editing**. A teaching method in which teacher and students work together to edit familiar, error-free text; the reciprocity of reading and writing is a key feature of interactive editing

**Interactive writing**. A teaching method in which students and teacher negotiate what they are going to write and then share the pen to construct the message

**Intonation**. Distinctive patterns of pitch in speaking that contribute to the meaning of phrases and sentences

**Key concepts**. The essential concepts to be taught/learned

**Key vocabulary**. The essential words to be taught/learned

**Leveling**. A method of determining a gradient of difficulty of texts used for instruction; used mostly in the primary grades

**Literacy centers**. Independent tasks or activities that support classroom learning and require no teacher assistance; centers are used in classrooms as a way of managing small group reading activities

**Literacy skills checklist**. A checklist of skills from reading and/or writing for use by a teacher or observer

# Glossary (continued)

**Literature response logs.** Student journals used for responding to ideas prompted by reading text

**Monitoring.** The act of self-evaluating reading and writing

**Narrative.** A story that can be true or fictional

**Nonfiction.** A form of literature based on fact

**Onset.** Usually the consonants preceding the vowel of a syllable

**Oral presentation.** A teaching method that provides direct instruction to prepare students to orally share information and ideas in a variety of settings

**Persuasive writing.** A style of writing used to convince a person to take an action or accept a point of view

**Phoneme.** Minimal sound unit of speech that when contrasted with another phoneme affects the meaning of a word

**Phonemic awareness.** The awareness of the sounds (phonemes) that make up spoken words

**Phonics.** The relationship between sounds (phonemes) and letters (graphemes)

**Pocket chart.** A tool used for instruction that has clear pockets to place letters, words, phrases, or sentences

**Prefix.** An affix attached before a root word

**Problem.** The basic conflict in a story

**Problem resolution.** The solution or outcome of the conflict in a story

**Problem solving strategies.** Mental operations that are used to do work while reading or writing

**Prompt.** Language used by the teacher to draw the student's attention to a particular aspect of the reading process

**Quantitative information.** Research using numerical terms to measure or describe

**Read aloud.** A teaching method for sharing a story aloud, developing vocabulary, modeling structure and fluency, and introducing content

**Readability.** A formula for determining the difficulty of a text using sentence length and syllable count

**Reciprocal teaching.** A teaching strategy whereby teacher and students share the responsibility for conducting a discussion

**Record of Oral Reading.** An account of a student's reading behaviors recorded during the oral reading of a text

**Remedial education.** A service specifically designed for students below grade level in achievement

**Rhyme.** Words that sound the same but do not necessarily look the same (for example, *date*, *eight*)

**Rime.** Words that sound the same and look the same (for example, in *cat*, *fat*, *at* is the rime)

**Root word.** The basic part of a word that carries the meaning

**Rubric.** A scoring convention or guide for writing that uses samples of expected student writing at that level to evaluate form, mechanics, and content

**Sentence stem.** Any of a number of basic sentence component types in a language

**Sentence strips**. Paper strips, generally six to nine inches wide, used to record writing of sentences

**Setting**. Location of a story or event

**Shared reading**. A teaching method in which the teacher and students read together from a text that is visible to all, to help develop reading strategies, increase fluency, and extend phonological awareness

**Sight words**. Words automatically recognized as a whole that do not require word analysis for identification

**Sources of information**. Any of the various sources that may assist in identifying a word not recognized at first glance; includes all aspects of phonics, structural analysis, syntax, and meaning

**Special education**. Specially designed instruction and related services provided to students with disabilities

**Story events**. The essential plot elements in the sequence of a story

**Story mapping**. Making an outline or graphic organizer of the elements of a story, such as character or plot

**Suffix**. An affix attached at the end of a root word

**Syllables**. Minimal units of sequential speech sounds, including a vowel or a vowel-consonant combination

**Task cards**. Teacher- or publisher-made cards for specific tasks for a center or independent activity

**Teaching points**. Instructional choices by the teacher, based on observing student problem solving

**Text comprehension**. The ability to take meaning from text

**Text density**. The amount of print on a page or section of material

**Text features**. Features found in print, including captions, pictures, glossaries, and other support for information

**Think aloud**. To model thinking behaviors to students by talking through a process as it is happening

**Venn diagram**. A graphic organizer used to compare and contrast

**Vocabulary**. The words needed to communicate

**Wikki Stix**. A commercially made product using wax-covered string that can be used to highlight letters, words, parts of speech, punctuation, etc.

**Word analysis**. A general label for analyzing words into their constituent parts

**Word, phrase, sentence level**. Different linguistic levels used for reading support and prompting

**Word bank**. A group of words used as a resource for reading and writing, usually posted in large print on a wall

**Word wall**. The use of print on walls that includes various types of words organized for instruction; high frequency words, word families or rhyming words, content area words, etc.

**Written language conventions**. The mechanics of writing, including punctuation, spelling, and other elements that impact meaning

# Bibliography

Adams, M. (1990). *Beginning to Read: Thinking and Learning about Print.* Cambridge, MA: MIT Press.

Adams, M. (1998). *Phonemic Awareness in Young Children.* Baltimore, MA: Paul H.Brookes Publishing Co.

Armbruster, B. B., Lehr, F., & Osborn, J. (2001). *Put Reading First: The Research Building Blocks for Teaching Children to Read.* Jessup, MD: United States Department of Education Publication Center.

Anderson, R.C. (1996). *Research Foundations to Support Wide Reading.* In Creany, V. (Ed.), *Promoting Reading in Developing Countries,* (pp. 44-77). Newark, DE: International Reading Association.

Bear, D., Invernizzi, M., Templeton, S., & Johnston, F. (1996). *Words Their Way.* Upper Saddle River, NJ: Prentice-Hall, Inc.

Beck, I., McKeown, M.G., Hamilton, R.L., & Kucan, L. (1998, Spring). "Getting at the Meaning." *American Educator,* 22(1), (pp. 66-85).

*Vocabulary Instructional Techniques.* In McKeown, M.G. & Curtis, M.E. (Eds.), *The Nature of Vocabulary Acquisition,* (pp. 147-163). Hillsdale, NJ: Erlbaum.

Blum, I.H., & Koskinen, P.S. (1991, Summer). "Repeated Reading: A Strategy for Enhancing Fluency and Fostering Expertise." *Theory Into Practice,* 30, (pp. 195-200).

Brady, S., & Moats, L.C. (1997). *Informed Instruction for Reading Success: Foundations for Teacher Preparation.* Baltimore, MD: Orton Dyslexia Society.

Bruner, J.S. (1983). *Child's Talk: Learning to Use Language.* London: W.W. Norton & Co.

Button, K., Johnson, M.J., & Furgerson, P. (1996). "Interactive Writing in a Primary Classroom." *The Reading Teacher,* 49(6), (pp. 446-454).

California Department of Education. (1998). *English Language Arts Content Standards for California Public Schools.* Sacramento, CA.

Chomsky, C. (1976). "After Decoding: What?" *Language Arts,* 53(3), (pp 288-96, 314).

Chomsky, C. (1972). "Stages in Language Development and Reading Exposure." *Harvard Educational Review,* 42(1), (pp. 1-33).

Clark, C.H. (1995). "Teaching Students about Reading: A Fluency Example." *Reading Horizons,* 35(3), (pp. 250-266).

Clay, M.M. (1991a). *Becoming Literate: The Construction of Inner Control.* Auckland, NZ: Heinemann.

Clay, M.M. (1991b, December). "Introducing a New Storybook to Young Readers." *The Reading Teacher,* 45, (pp. 264-273).

Cunningham, A.E., & Stanovich, K.E. (1998, Spring). "What Reading Does for the Mind." *American Educator,* 22(1), (pp. 8-15).

Ehri, L.C. (1998). "The Development of Spelling Knowledge and Its Role in Reading Acquisition and Reading Disability." *Journal of Reading Disabilities,* 22(6), (pp. 356-365).

Fletcher, J., & Lyon, R. (1998). *Reading: A Research-based Approach.* In W. Evers (Ed.), *What's Gone Wrong in America's Classrooms.* Palo Alto, CA: Hoover Institution Press, Stanford University.

Foorman, B.R., Francis, D.J., Fletcher, J.M., Schatschneider, C., & Metha, P. (1998). "The Role of Instruction in Learning to Read: Preventing Reading Failure in At-risk Children." *Journal of Educational Psychology,* 90, (pp. 1-15).

Foorman, B.R., Francis, D.J., Shaywitz, S.E., Shaywitz, B., & Fletcher, J.M. (1997). *The Case for Early Reading Intervention.* In B. Blachman (Ed.), *Foundations of Reading Acquisition: Implications for Intervention and Dyslexia.* Hillsdale, NJ: Lawrence Erlbaum.

Fry, E. (1997). *Comprehensive Phonics Charts. Phonics Charts.* California: Laguna Beach Educational Books.

Fry, E. (1977). *Elementrary Reading Instruction.* New York, NY: McGraw Hill.

Hasbrouck, J.E., & Tindal, G. (1992, Spring). "Curriculum-based Oral Reading Fluency Norms for Students in Grades 2 through 5." *Teaching Exceptional Children,* 24, (pp. 41-44).

Heald-Taylor, B.G. (1998, February). "Three Paradigms of Spelling Instruction in Grades 3 to 6." *The Reading Teacher,* 51(5), (pp. 404-413).

Henry, M.K. (1988). "Beyond Phonics: Integrated Decoding and Spelling Instruction Based on Word Origin and Structure." *Annals of Dyslexia,* 38, (pp. 258-275).

Hiebert, E.H. (1988, November). "The Role of Literacy Experiences in Early Childhood Programs." *Elementary School Journal,* 89, (pp. 161-171).

Invernizzi, M.A., Abouzeid, M.P., & Bloodgood, J.W. (1997, March). "Integrated Word Study: Spelling, Grammar, and Meaning in the Language Arts Classroom." *Language Arts,* 74, (pp. 185-192).

Juel, C. (1988). "Learning to Read and Write: A Longitudinal Study of 54 Children from First through Fourth Grades." *Journal of Educational Psychology,* 80(4), (pp. 437-447).

Kirk, S., Kirk, W., & Minskoff, E. (1985). *Phonic Remedial Reading Lessons.* Novata, CA: Academic Therapy Publications.

Liberman, I.Y., Shankweiler, D., & Liberman (Eds.) (1989). *Phonology and Reading Disability: Solving the Reading Puzzle.* Ann Arbor, MI: University of Michigan Press.

Lyon, G.R., & Moats, L.C. (1997, November/December). "Critical Conceptual and Methodological Considerations in Reading Intervention Research." *Journal of Learning Disabilities*, 30, (pp. 578-588).

Moats, L.C. (1998). *Reading, Spelling, and Writing Disabilities in the Middle Grades*. In B. Wong (Ed.), *Learning About Learning Disabilities*. San Diego, CA: Academic Press.

Moats, L.C. (1994). "The Missing Foundation in Teacher Education: Knowledge of the Structure of Spoken and Written Language." *Annals of Dyslexia: An Interdisciplinary Journal of the Orton Dyslexia Society*, 44, (p. 81).

Nathan, R.G., & Stanovich, K.E. (1991, Summer). "The Causes and Consequences of Differences in Reading Fluency." *Theory Into Practice*, 30, (pp. 176-184).

Pearson, P.D., Roehler, L.R., Dole, J.A., & Duffy, G.G. (1992). *Developing Expertise in Reading Comprehension*. In Samuels, S.J., & Farstrup, A.E. (Eds.), *What Research Says to the Teachers*, (pp. 145-199). Newark, DE: International Reading Association.

Perfetti, C. (1995). "Cognitive Research Can Inform Reading Education." *Journal of Research in Reading*, 18, (pp. 106-115).

Samuels, S.J. (1997, February). "The Method of Repeated Readings." *The Reading Teacher*, 50(5), (pp. 376-384).

Samuels, S.J., Schermer, N., & Reinking, D. (1992). *Reading Fluency: Techniques for Making Decoding Automatic*. In S. Samuels and A. Farstrup (Eds.), *What Research Has to Say about Reading Instruction*, (pp. 124-144). Newark, DE: International Reading Association.

Shaywitz, S.E. (1996). "Dyslexia." *Scientific American*, 275(5), (pp. 98-104).

Snow, C. E., Burns, S. M., & Griffin, P. (Eds.). (1998). *Preventing Reading Difficulties in Young Children*. Washington, D.C.: National Academy Press.

Stahl, S.A., & Shiel, T.G. (1992). "Teaching Meaning Vocabulary: Productive Approaches for Poor Readers." *Reading and Writing Quarterly: Overcoming Learning Disabilities*, 8, (pp. 223-241).

Swartz, S.L., Klein, A.F., & Shook, R.E. (2001). *Interactive Writing and Interactive Editing*. Carlsbad, CA: Dominie Press.

Swartz, S.L., Shook, R.E., & Klein, A.F. (2002). *Shared Reading: Reading with Children*. Carlsbad, CA: Dominie Press.

Swartz, S.L., Shook, R.E., & Klein, A.F. (2002). *Foundation for California Early Literacy Learning (Technical Report)*. Redlands, CA: Foundation for California Early Literacy Learning.

Tangel, D., & Blachman, B. (1995, June). "Effect of Phoneme Awareness Instruction on the Invented Spellings of First Grade Children: A One-year Follow-up." *Journal of Reading Behavior*, 27, (pp. 153-185).

Tomlinson, C.A., & Kalbfleisch, M.L. (1998, November). "Teach Me, Teach My Brain: A Call for Differentiated Classrooms." *Educational Leadership*, 56(3), (pp. 52-55).

Torgesen, J.K. (1998, Spring/Summer). "Catch Them before the Fall." *American Educator*, 22(1), (pp. 32-39).

Torgesen, J.K., Wagner, R.K., Y Rashotte, C.A. (1997). *Approaches to the Prevention and Remediation of Phonologically-based Disabilities*. In B. Blachman (Ed.), *Foundations of Reading Acquisition and Dyslexia: Implications for Early Intervention*, (pp. 287-304) Mahwah, NJ: Lawrence Erlbaum.

Triplett, C.F., & Stahl, S.A. (1998, Summer). "Words, Words, Words. Word Sorts: Maximizing Student Input in Work Study." *Illinois Reading Council Journal*, 26(3), (pp. 84-87).

Washington D.C.: National Center of Education and the Economy and the University of Pittsburgh. (1999). *Reading and Writing Grade by Grade: Primary Literacy Standards for Kindergarten through Third Grade*.

Washington D.C.: National Institute of Child Health and Human Development: Report of the National Reading Panel (2001). *Teaching Children to Read: An Evidence-Based Assessment of the Scientific Research Literature on Reading and Its Implications for Reading Instruction*.

Weir, C. (1998, March). "Using Embedded Questions to Jumpstart Metacognition in Middle School Remedial Readers." *Journal of Adolescent & Adult Literacy*, 41(6), (pp. 458-467).

Wolfe, P. (1998, November). "Revisiting Effective Teaching." *Educational Leadership*, 56(3), (pp. 61-64).

Zutell, J. (1996, October). "The Directed Spelling Thinking Activity (DSTA): Providing an Effective Balance in Work Study Instruction." *The Reading Teacher*, 50(2), (pp. 98-108).

# Index

Acrostic, 107, 128

Alphabetic principle, 54, 96

Anthology, 78

Artifacts, 124, 126

Assessment, 8, 12, 13, 14, 131

Background knowledge, 3, 14, 29, 34, 38, 39, 40, 47, 94

Bar graph, 90, 91, 102

Book clubs, 4, 5, 120, 139

Characters, 18, 24, 25, 26, 28, 29, 31, 38, 53, 54, 62, 72, 81, 84, 107, 114, 115,120, 123, 126, 133, 136, 138

Cinquain, 128

Clip art, 64, 66, 87, 116, 119, 129

Collaborative model, v, 1, 48

Concepts of print, 100

Correction, 50, 131, 138

Decode, 2, 3, 4, 7, 26, 36, 39, 49, 133, 137

Disability(ies), 1, 48

English language learners, v, 1, 2, 3, 4, 13, 39

Fiction, 14, 16, 18, 20, 22, 24, 26, 28, 30, 32, 34, , 54, 81, 136, 137

Fluency, 1, 3, 11, 24, 50, 54, 74, 76, 77, 78, 80, 131, 135, 138

Format, 100, 114, 120, 122, 125

Frustration reading level, 138

Graphic organizer, 54, 62, 102, 103, 112, 119, 123

Haiku, 128

High frequency words, 13, 16, 18, 20, 22, 23, 24, 26, 30, 32, 34, 54, 58, 74, 78, 99, 108, 112, 118, 134

Inclusion, v, 1, 49, 48

Independent reading, 4, 5, 11, 49, 53, 68, 83, 120

Independent reading level, 6

Independent writing, 83, 102, 112

Informational text, 88, 90, 91, 100

Instructional reading level, 6

Interactive editing, 48, 66, 84, 102, 103, 108, 111, 116, 125

Interactive writing, 4, 8, 12, 48, 49, 62, 68, 71, 72, 73, 76, 82, 84, 92, 100, 102, 104, 106, 108, 110, 111, 112, 114, 116, 122, 124, 126, 128

Key concepts, 102, 125

Key vocabulary, 84, 118

Literacy centers, v, 1, 8, 9, 11, 12, 48, 57, 58, 59

Literacy Skills Checklist, 8, 13, 131, 132

Monitoring, 5, 50, 53, 94

Narrative, 22, 25, 33, 54, 73, 102, 104, 123, 125, 126

Nonfiction, 12, 14, 16, 18, 19, 20, 21, 22, 24, 26, 28, 30, 31, 32, 34, 35, 36, 53, 54, 102, 104, 105, 118, 120

Oral presentation, 52, 79, 116, 124, 125

Persuasive writing, 100

Phonics, v, 1, 3, 4, 7, 9, 40, 49, 50, 54, 66, 71, 112

Phonemic awareness, 3, 64

Pocket chart, 66, 70, 72, 78, 79, 87, 96, 119

Problem solving strategies, 5, 48, 86, 94

Prompt, 5, 6, 7, 9, 10, 30, 32, 48, 49, 50, 51, 52, 74, 96, 120, 131, 139

Readability, 36, 37

Read aloud, 62, 75, 76, 80, 82, 84, 88, 92, 94, 96, 104, 110, 111, 120, 122, 124, 128

Reciprocal teaching, 4, 5

Record of Oral Reading, 6, 8, 11, 14, 131

Remedial education, 1

Rhyme, 65, 66, 72, 80, 124

Rime, 24, 25, 50, 66, 67, 71, 74, 108, 112, 113

Root word, 34, 68, 69, 111

Rubric, 39, 62, 74, 76, 118, 119, 125

Sentence strips, 72, 78, 87, 111, 112, 119

Shared reading, 4, 5, 6, 8, 12, 49, 62, 66, 68, 70, 71, 72, 73, 76, 78, 80, 82, 84, 88, 90, 92, 100, 102, 108, 112, 114, 116, 122

Sight words, 17, 19

Sources of information, 1, 5, 9, 26, 40, 49, 51, 70, 71

Special education, v, 1, 48, 49, 57

Story mapping, 121, 123

Syllables, 37, 65, 68, 106, 107, 112

Task cards, 68, 86, 106, 109

Teaching points, 7, 11, 52, 53, 54, 126

Text comprehension, 3, 4, 50, 53, 54

Text features, 12, 36, 54, 104, 105

Think aloud, 120

Venn diagram, 102, 103

Word analysis, 1, 7, 9, 107

Word bank, 82, 83, 84, 87, 96, 97, 99, 107, 108, 110, 111

Word wall, 71, 99, 106, 108, 112, 113

Written language conventions, 114, 116, 118